Wesleyan Methodism

Exploring Methodism

Wesleyan Methodism

John Munsey Turner

EPWORTH PRESS

British Library Cataloguing in Publication data

A catalogue record for this book is available
from the British Library

0 7162 0590 4

First published in 2005
by Epworth Press
4 John Wesley Road
Werrington
Peterborough PE4 6ZP

Typeset by Rowland Phototypesetting Ltd,
Bury St Edmunds, Suffolk
Printed and bound in Great Britain by
Biddles Ltd, *www.biddles.co.uk*

Contents

Preface

Anyone who writes on Methodism after Wesley must express a huge debt to historians such as Henry Rack, John Walsh, John Kent, Reginald Ward, John Bowmer, Michael Watts, David Bebbington and Hugh McLeod – to mention but a few – who have revolutionised our picture of the nineteenth-century Free Churches. Their work goes alongside significant local histories and biographies. I sincerely hope I have not plagiarised any of them, though their research and insights will be obvious in this short book. I have also pillaged my own books and articles with the risk of being accused of repeating myself. I have assumed a general readership rather than professional historians. I have tried, also, not to repeat what has already been written in the previous volumes in this series especially those on *Theology* (Thomas Langford), *Spirituality* (Gordon Wakefield), *Primitive Methodism* (Geoffrey Milburn) and the forthcoming volume on *Overseas Missions* (Robert Dolman).

It is a matter of controversy whether historians should seek to be 'relevant', but we cannot pretend that we do not write from a particular context. So I have asked some questions which we cannot help asking at the beginning of the twenty-first century. There are gaps, of course, some due to ignorance, others to sheer lack of space. Some may see it as a view from the Midlands and the North, but this is where much of my life has been spent. Oral history is important, too, in assessing Methodist history, so I have used my own ancestral roots in Wales and ministry in Colchester, Burton upon Trent, Sheffield, Leeds, Birmingham, Halifax and Bolton, and my upbringing in Wolverhampton, which represent some of the 'many Methodisms'.

John Munsey Turner

Preface

Introduction

The 300th anniversary of John Wesley's birth in the Rectory at Epworth, in Lincolnshire, on 17 June 1703 brought this remarkable eighteenth-century man to the forefront again. Do we still think of him as the little Church of England priest, who got on his horse in 1738, riding off in six directions at once like one of Stephen Leacock's heroes, preaching 40,000 sermons on the way? The 'myths' often hide the man.

The Evangelical Revival was well under way in Europe, America and Wales before Wesley plugged into it, realising ordinary people's desire for a 'religion of the heart'. Wesley's context was the Great Britain of the early industrial revolution with the population doubling in his lifetime. The Church of England was unable to cope with the areas of swift demographic change. Voluntary religion filled the gaps, with Wesley, who was a superb pragmatist, sensing the need for more than the Religious Societies, which were a feature of parishes like that of his father – and his mother, who played a lively role when her husband was away. Wesley saw the need for a 'ginger group' to stir up the church and reach those outside it. His aim was to preach 'plain truth to plain people'.

His own experience of personal faith and assurance, which occurred on 24 May 1738 when he heard a reading from the Reformer, Martin Luther, at a Religious Society in Aldersgate Street, London, was clearly decisive. It enabled him to combine conviction that salvation was available to all, not just an elect few, with what we can call a 'catholic' style of concern for growth and holiness, perfect love of God and humanity. He soon realised that unless his preaching in the open air, begun in April 1739, led to the setting up of 'societies' and smaller groups, it would be a 'rope of sand'. Here his skill in organisation is clear. The 'class meeting', or 'cell' as we call it now, was the means by which people could find faith and grow in it. The class would meet normally each week under lay leaders, who would soon include women. Smaller 'bands' would take in those moving on to perfection. The classes would unite in societies in local areas. The members of the societies were expected to attend their parish church for Morning and Evening Prayer and Holy Communion, which was usually celebrated monthly in towns, quarterly elsewhere.

New groups tend to develop their own 'feasts and

---

1. *Wesley's summaries of doctrine 1746, 1790*

Our main doctrines, which include all the rest, are three, that of repentance of faith and of holiness. The first of these we account, as it were, the porch of religion; the next the door; the third religion itself.

I am glad Brother D— has more light with regard to full sanctification. This doctrine is the grand depositum, which God has lodged with the people called Methodists; and for the sake of propagating this chiefly He appeared to have raised us up.

Source: R. E. Davies (ed.), *The Works of John Wesley*, vol. 9, Nashville: Abingdon, 1989, p. 227. See also, J. Telford (ed.), *The Letters of John Wesley*, London: Epworth Press, 1960, vol. 2, p. 268; vol. 8, p. 238. (To Robert Carr Brackenbury.)

fasts'. This soon happened in Wesley's 'Connexion' as he called it. The *Preaching Service* would combine sermon, extempore prayer and the singing of Charles Wesley's hymns. This was controlled fervour. Wesley could not help comparing it with what he experienced in some parish churches.

---

2. *Even Wesley got bored at worship! 1757*

The longer I am absent from London and the more I attend the service of the church in other places the more I am convinced of the unspeakable advantage which the people called Methodists enjoy; I mean even with regard to public worship, particularly on the Lord's Day . . . the persons who assemble there are not a gay, giddy crowd, who come chiefly to see and be seen; nor a company of goodly, formal, outside Christians, whose religion lies in a dull round of duties . . . Nor are their solemn addresses to God interrupted either by the formal drawl of a parish clerk, the screaming of boys who bawl out what they neither feel nor understand, or the unseasonable and unmeaning impertinence of a voluntary on the organ. When it is seasonable to sing praise to God, they do it with the spirit and with the understanding also; not in the miserable, scandalous doggerel of Hopkins and Sternhold, but in psalms and hymns which are both sense and poetry, such as would sooner provoke a critic to turn Christian than a Christian to turn critic.

Source: J. Telford (ed.), *The Letters of John Wesley*, London: Epworth Press, 1960, vol. 3, pp. 226–7.

There were other 'prudential means of grace' as Wesley called them. *The Love-feast*, borrowed from the Moravians, became a democratic folk meal with bread and water handed round using a common cup, with testimonies and hymns. *The Covenant Service*, derived from the Puritans of the previous century, stressed an annual personal and corporate rededication of life. *The Watchnight* was a kind of vigil usually on the night of the full moon – less risk of being 'mugged' on the way home. We shall look more at how the means of grace developed later.

Wesley needed quickly the use of a young group

---

3. *Dr Joseph Beaumont reflects on Wesley 1834*

Mr Wesley, like a strong and skilful rower, looked one way while every stroke of his oar took him in the opposite direction. He never resolved that he would go further than the church. We must have room to breathe and move our arms.

Source: Benjamin Gregory, *Sidelight on the Conflicts of Methodism*, London: Cassell, 1898, p. 161.

---

of itinerant preachers, under his strict direction, and locally based people who became the 'local preachers'. The itinerants developed into a presbyterate after Wesley's death. The societies were grouped into 'circuits', often at first very large, with an itinerant preacher as 'assistant' to Wesley. In 1744, and afterwards, Wesley gathered a Conference of his preachers, which was legalised in 1784. 'Preaching Houses' (Wesley's term) began to be built, and reluctantly registered, as dissenting places of worship under the Toleration Act, which protected them from the mob. Even if Wesley always affirmed – if highly critical – that he had no wish to leave the Church of England, his actions made separation probable. His loyalty was not helped by mob action, sometimes stirred up by hostile clergy and the feeling of some bishops that there was a danger of fanaticism ('enthusiasm') and chaos. The historian Macaulay[1] wrote that the Pope would have put a monk's cowl on him, setting him free. There was something of the feel of medieval friars about the early itinerants.

Wesley was clearly authoritarian in his control of his Connexion. He was no democrat, although at local level there was considerable lay autonomy, which could spill over later into local and national life. He soon had his headquarters at London, Bristol and Newcastle. His carefully planned journeys in horseback – later he used a chaise – took place mainly between March and November, including visits to the West Country and Ireland. By his death there were 72,000 members of the Methodist Societies, about as many as there were Roman Catholics at that time.

John Wesley was a man of his age – his strong

4. *John Henry Newman reflects*

Methodism and Popery are in different ways the refuge of those whom the church stints of the means of grace – they are the foster mothers of abandoned children. The neglect of the daily service, the desecration of festivals, the Eucharist scantily administered, insubordination permitted in all ranks of the Church, orders and offices imperfectly developed, the want of Societies for particular religious objects, and the like deficiencies lead the feverish mind, desirous of a vent to its feelings, and a stricter rule of life, to the small religious Communities, to prayer and bible meetings, and ill-advised institutions and societies on the one hand – on the other to the solemn and captivating services by which Popery gains its proselytes.

Source: Advertisement to the *Tracts for the Times*, Oxford 1834–41, in A. O. J. Cockshut (ed.), *Religious Controversies of the Nineteenth Century: Selected Documents*, London: Methuen, 1966, p. 62.

rejection of slavery certainly shows an Enlightenment aspect. His last letter was to support William Wilberforce in his battle against the slave trade and slavery itself.

Wesley's desire for a 'Community of Goods'[2] among his people never entirely left him. At the end of his life, he tramped through the London snow on a one man 'Christian Aid' campaign for the poor. Indeed he said: 'I bear the rich, I love the poor.' Unlike many, he did not blame the poor for their poverty or attribute it to their idleness, but at the same time he quoted 'cleanliness is next to Godliness', taking delight in making some of the turbulent poor, industrious and sober, with the sermon slogan 'gain all you can, save all you can, give all you can'. The appeal in the end was to the industrious sort of people. The chapel would become an alternative to the pub and wild folk customs, and attractive to women.

Wesley had been called a 'both . . . and' man.[3] He combined evangelistic fervour with disciplined control. He was able to accommodate popular fervour without giving way to its most bizarre manifestations, though these did occur. Though he was an Evangelical, he had a passionate love of Holy Communion, and his use of the spirituality of Roman Catholics and the Early Church Fathers was unusual for his time.

He was a man of the Enlightenment, experimenting on the sick with electric shocks! He was also a believer in special providences, very chary of giving any credence to the Voltaires of this world. If he was Anglican in his combination of scripture, tradition (including the Anglican Reformers such as Cranmer) and reason, he added a need for experience, which linked him both with some philosophy, especially that of John Locke, and the Moravians. He broke with the latter over the doctrine of Christian Perfection. He was a pioneer of cheap publishing – *The Christian Library* was a 'Reader's Digest' of spirituality from all sources, but with Wesleyan 'spin' – it was hardly a bestseller! An Oxford don to the end, he was also able to communicate clearly in the market place. He had great charm, energy and charisma, but could be accused of a love of power. Formidable ladies such as the

5. *Wesley to Wilberforce, 24 February 1791*

Unless the divine power has raised you up to be an *Athanasius Contra Mundum* [Athanasius against the world] I do not see how you can go through your glorious enterprise in opposing that execrable villainy which is the scandal of religion, of England and of human nature . . . Go on in the name of God and in the power of his might, till even American slavery (the vilest that even saw the sun) shall vanish away before it. Reading this morning a tract written by a poor African, I was particularly struck by that circumstance that a man who has a black skin being wronged or estranged by a white man can have no redress; it being a *law* in all our colonies that the *oath* of a black against a white goes for nothing. What villainy is this?

Source: J. Telford (ed.), *The Letters of John Wesley*, London: Epworth Press, 1960, vol. 8, p. 265.

Countess of Huntingdon did not accept his authority and was told once to 'use her reason'. Her reply, at a time of great evangelical disputing, was that he 'was a heretic'.[4] Vivian Green was accurate enough when he said that 'his charm cloaked an iron will, he was granite in aspic'.[5] Certainly he was one of the great characters of the eighteenth century – but what then? That is our story.

I

After Wesley – the Era of Revolution 1791–1820

Wesley's legacy

John Wesley died on 3 March 1791. *The Gentleman's Magazine*, which had previously been critical, in a long obituary said: 'As a man and a writer, he must be considered one of the most extraordinary characters that this or any age has produced'. At the same time, one of Wesley's itinerant preachers, John Pawson (1737–1806), whom Wesley had ordained for work in Scotland in 1785, was realistic but also full of foreboding.

---

6. Wesley's death

This will surely be a time of general mourning as the Lord has taken our Master from our head . . . I am glad that the dear good old man did not outlive his usefulness . . . His death has certainly brought us into a very different situation than we ever were before. But yet I think he had lived just as long as he could be useful; had he lived much longer, designing men might have taken advantage of his weakness and have done wrong things by his authority, and so sheltered themselves under his wings. His death was well timed and glorious and we have good reason to praise God that it was so.

Source: J. C. Bowmer and John A. Vickers, *The Letters of John Pawson*, vol. 1, London: Methodist Publishing House, 1994, pp. 96, 99; March, April, 1791.

Pawson, and others, saw three possibilities for the Methodist 'Connexion' which we can define as a distinctive style of religious organisation, neither sect nor yet denomination, but holding together styles of spirituality, fellowship and mission, with itinerant preachers set apart for the task of evangelism at first, but then acting as a shuttle, weaving a close community, which next century called itself the 'Body'. The first possibility was *The Old Plan* – continuing allegiance to the Church of England, forbidding the itinerant preachers to preside at Holy Communion in the meeting houses. This was a view put forward by Methodist laymen at Hull and held by the formidable Joseph Benson (1748–1821).

The second possibility was *The New Plan* – becoming an independent denomination with the preachers acting virtually as ordained ministers. Samuel Bradburn (1751–1816) took this line, acting upon it at Bristol to the distaste of the local Evangelical vicar, as well as some Methodists. Pawson advocated *'following Providence'* which would involve a pragmatic approach. It would lead fairly rapidly, but not without sour and bitter conflict, especially in Bristol, to what was virtually The New Plan. There was to be a small but highly significant schism, *The Methodist New Connexion* of 1797, of those who wanted total independence with a Conference consisting of an equal number of itinerant preachers and lay representatives, which finally came about in Wesleyanism in 1878.

---

7. Church or no church? Alexander Kilham

It appears that our being closely united to the Established Church is founded on reasons not justified from the Scriptures. It is more honourable to attend service at the Church than to worship among the Dissenters! It takes away a good deal of the scandal of the cross. It may be advantageous to our business in the world . . . our being so closely united with the Church cannot be looked on in any other light than a specious trimming between God and the world. We never met with any argument for our continuing closely united with the Church, but what are political or, in other words, carnal and sold under sin.

Source: George Smith, *History of Wesleyan Methodism*, vol. 2, 5th ed., C. H. Kelly, pp. 45–6 from Alexander Kilham, *An Address to the Members and Friends of the Newcastle Society*, Newcastle, 1792.

So let us ask these questions. What did Wesley leave behind? How did his legacy lead to the creation of the Wesleyan Methodist Connexion, not to speak of the 'many Methodisms' in America, and rapidly in many parts of the second British Empire and beyond? Wesley always claimed to be a 'Church of England man' and priest. He never wished to leave his native church and was not officially thrust out of it. His policy, however, of unlimited mission – 'I look upon all the world as my parish' (1739) – soon involved, as we have seen, holding religious meetings unauthorised by the parish parsons, the creation of 'societies' outside the parish system and ultimately the building of Preaching Houses (later to be called chapels) for meetings and worship. In 1784 there were 300 such meeting houses, with what we have called the feasts and fasts, which follow the setting up of any religious group.

Wesley still wished his people to go to the parish churches. But, in 1781, the Conference urged people to leave if the clergy preached 'the absolute decrees' (i.e. Calvinism) and ridiculed Christian perfection. Services could be held in 'church hours' if the priest is a 'notoriously wicked man' or 'when he preaches Arian or any equally pernicious doctrine' or if there is no church within two or three miles. Many of the groups sucked into the Methodist Connexion were dissenting in style with no real links with the church.

The registration of the Preaching Houses under the Toleration Act, though disliked by Wesley, was a further sign of separation. The official legal setting up of the Conference, which had first met in 1744, by the *Deed of Declaration* of 1784 with the 'legal hundred' itinerant preachers who ratified Conference decisions, assured Methodism's survival after Wesley's death. This remained the norm in Wesleyanism until Methodist union in 1932. The *Model Deed* of 1763 laid down who might preach in the chapels with Wesley's *Forty Four Sermons* and *Notes on the New Testament* as 'standards for preaching', a matter still observed by preachers, who are bidden to preach 'our doctrines'.

The war of Independence in America led to the provision of a church constitution for the Methodists in what had become the USA. Ministers were ordained in America by Dr Thomas Coke (1747–1814), an Anglican priest, who had been appointed 'Superintendent' by Wesley. He and Francis Asbury called themselves bishops, which annoyed Wesley. A revised Prayer Book was especially designed for America, then for Great Britain and the Mission Field. There followed the controversial ordination of ministers serving in Scotland. Mgr Ronald Knox, mischievously, called them 'Gretna Green ordinations' which, unlike Gretna Green marriages, were not to be normative south of the border, a matter which also annoyed John Pawson, who was one of them. There followed ordinations for the colonies and finally for England. There is the clear possibility that Wesley contemplated some form of episcopacy for England, although the Conference in 1794 rejected any idea that the Chairmen of Districts, who assumed office in 1792, should act as bishops. If there were to be bishop-like figures, they would be the Superintendents (formerly 'Assistants' to Wesley) of the circuits, a matter still relevant to modern discussion about *episcopē* or oversight. They certainly acquired powers which many a bishop would envy.

The context

The 1780s had seen a considerable growth in the societies. There were 72,467 members in 1791 in Great Britain, with many more people developing close links. They came to be called 'adherents'. In the USA there were 76,000 members in 1791. Estimates suggest about as many Methodists as there were Roman Catholics outside Ireland. Both groups were destined for rapid expansion, as were the 'old dissenters' – Baptists and Independents – in the next generation, to the discomfiture of the Establishment, including the Evangelicals. There were, in 1791, 470 chapels in the 114 circuits with 300 full time itinerants and about 2,000 local preachers, who conducted a growing number of preaching services especially in the smaller societies. They were officially recognised with a Local Preachers' Meeting to be held in each circuit after 1796. About 60% of members were women, some of them quite formidable spinsters and widows, though many were domestic servants. There were many more housemaids than miners. The members were mainly not at the bottom of the social pyramid, even if comparatively poor, but normally they were those who had some slight social standing – artisans, small farmers, shop keepers. A little later it can be shown that 62% of male members were artisans, i.e. masons, shoemakers, cordwainers, saddlers, harness makers, carpenters, potters, croppers, stockingers and the like. Labourers represented 9.5% and colliers 7.6%.[1]

Most Methodists were in the West Riding of Yorkshire or the North East, Lancashire, the Midlands including the Potteries, Lincolnshire, the West Country and in some areas around London. There was, however, a 'Methodist desert' for another generation or more in the south, in Sussex, Surrey, Hampshire, Wiltshire and Berkshire. We shall analyse this later. There was, as yet, little specifically Arminian Methodist work in Wales, which was dominated by Calvinist groups, which became the Calvinistic Methodist Church in 1811, later to be called the Presbyterian Church of Wales. In Scotland, the large towns had some Methodist chapels, while in Ireland the 'linen triangle' in Ulster and the area around Enniskillen had strong Methodist groups.

Methodist strength in 1800 was largely in the gaps of the parish system: in areas of large parishes, especially in the north, in 'open' parishes not dominated by squire and parson; and new industrial villages as in Shropshire and around Bristol and Newcastle. In typical areas like Calderdale and Rossendale on the borders of Yorkshire and Lancashire, Wesley had made 'takeover' bids for growing religious groups, catering for people's need for a 'religion of the heart'. Halifax parish, for instance, was as large as Rutland. Even with 'chapels of ease', it was far too large to be pastorally efficient. Generalisations can be dangerous, since Methodism was strong in York, under the shadow of the Minster, and also in Huddersfield, where Anglican Evangelicalism was strong, though it had difficulty in securing pastoral continuity. Societies, too, could be bedevilled by conflict and could crumble, as membership figures show. In 1791 the largest circuits in membership were typified by Bradford, Leeds, Manchester, Liverpool, Sheffield, Bolton and Halifax. The cotton towns were growing fast – the parish of Manchester increased in population from 125,911 in 1801 to 515,581 in 1851. The same was true of the iron, steel and cutlery town, Sheffield, and the wool towns like Bradford, growing from 13,264 inhabitants in 1801 to 103,378 in 1851. From 1791 to 1850 the number of Wesleyan members increased from 72,476 to 358,277 with the greatest strength then in Yorkshire, Lancashire, County Durham, Northumberland, Middlesex and Cornwall. In 1801 the Wesleyans represented 0.85% of the population; by 1830 it was 1.53%. By 1881, it was no longer matching population growth. England's population was about 5 million in 1700, 9 million by 1800, 14 million in 1831 and 22 million by 1871.

Before we plunge into Wesleyan history, we need to be aware of a wider context. In 1789 the French Revolution broke out. Some Dissenters, such as Dr Richard Price, welcomed it. As young William Wordsworth naively cried:

Bliss was it in that dawn to be alive
But to be young was very heaven.

There was real fear of French Jacobin influence in Britain – the very idea of 'democracy' was associated with revolution. Bishop Horsley of Rochester – no fool – thought that Methodism was being infiltrated by Jacobins. In 1800 the Toleration Act, which had given Dissenters some freedom in 1689, just survived. Dr Thomas Coke, who tried and failed to found a Mission in Paris, feared those Dissenters who toasted revolution – 'a bloody summer and a headless king'. This explains some of the opposition to men such as Alexander Kilham (1762–98), who was advocating greater power for 'the people' in Methodism. He used the clichés of the radicals rather as the Liberation theologians, uncritically, used Marxist language in the 1970s, not realising that revolutions have a habit of devouring their children, producing a Napoleon then and Mugabe now.

Many times during the period of war against Napoleon, Conference declared its loyalty to king and constitution, sometimes concerned about its own survival. W. R. Ward did not exaggerate when he stated that

the generation overshadowed by the French revolution was the most important generation in the modern history not only of English religion but most of the Christian world. For the Revolution altered forever the terms on which religious establishments, the chief device on which the nations of the world relied for christianising the people, must work.[2]

We might add the growth of industry and urbanisation. It is in this context that Wesleyanism began to grow rapidly, as did the older dissenting groups, who developed itinerant styles very similar to those of the Wesleyans.

Becoming a denomination

So the Conference met frequently at times of war with France though their own affairs were an urgent priority. In 1791, a group of Methodist leaders issued what came to be called the Halifax Circular. Copying Scottish precedents, the President should be appointed annually, like the Moderator of the General Assembly of the Church of Scotland. Both

---

8. *The Halifax Circular, 30 March 1791*

There appear to us but two ways: either to appoint another King in Israel; or to be governed by the Conference Plan, by forming ourselves into committees. If you adopt the first, who is the man? What power is he to be invested with? And what revenue is he to be allowed? But this is incompatible with the *Conference Deed*. If the latter we take the liberty to offer our thought upon that subject.

1. Fill up the vacant places in the Conference Deed with Preachers, according to their *seniority in the work*.
2. Chuse [*sic*] a President for *one year only*, according to the enrolled Deed.
3. Appoint a secretary or stewards for one year only, except for the Preachers' Fund.
4. Appoint a person from year to year to hold a Conference in Ireland.
5. Appoint different committees who will take in all the circuits in three kingdoms to manage the affairs of their respective Districts from one Conference to another etc. etc.

The signatories included William Thompson, Superintendent at Halifax, President 1791; John Pawson (President 1793, 1801); and Christopher Hopper, who had presided over Conference in Wesley's absence.

Source: George Smith, *History*, vol. 2, pp. 688–9; R. E. Davies and G. Rupp (eds), *History of the Methodist Church in Great Britain* (HMGB), London: Epworth Press, 1988, vol. 4, pp. 241–2.

churches maintain this practice, allowing a great variety of styles of people to occupy the office.

From Hull came an assertion of the need to maintain relationships with the Church of England – Hull was a centre of Evangelicalism, typified by William Wilberforce. The people of Redruth, on the other hand, wanted far more involvement of lay people, a presage of problems to come. The Conference of 1791 had to act quickly.

---

9. *Our future economy 1791*

Question 8. What regulations are necessary for the preservation of our whole economy, as the Rev. Mr. Wesley left it?
A. Let the three kingdoms be divided into Districts; England into nineteen; Scotland into two; . . . and Ireland into six . . .

Question 24. It is necessary to enter into any arrangements in respect of our future economy?
A. We engage to follow strictly the plan, which Mr. Wesley left us at his death.

Source: *Minutes of Conference*, 1791. HMGB, vol. 4, p. 245.

What precisely was 'the Plan' which Mr Wesley left? Between 1791 and 1795 there was considerable difficulty in deciding what the 'providential way' really was. Ordinations continued, but were forbidden in 1792. Distinctions between the 'ordained' and 'unordained' itinerant preachers were to end – no gowns or 'reverends'. This was not a 'low' view of ministry so much as a desire not to appear to be a new form of Dissent. Soon, the idea spread that 'reception into full Connexion' by the Conference, the form of accepting men into itinerant ministry, was tantamount to ordination.

Preachers accepted the title 'Reverend' in 1818; ordination by the traditional laying on of hands was introduced by Wesleyanism in 1836. Matters of ordination and celebrating the Lord's Supper in chapels were decided by lot, with Dr Adam Clarke (1760–1832) standing on a table announcing that the sacrament was not to be celebrated in chapels! This style of decision-making could not continue. By 1795 the 'lot' was laid aside, the Plan of Pacification making it clear that the sacrament could be celebrated in chapels by the itinerants, provided that the trustees and leaders agreed. Instructions were given as to the liturgy to be used, though we must remember that Conference directions were not always obeyed to the letter.

The Plan of Pacification (see Box 10) effectively marks the separation of Methodism from the Church of England, even if there was a rule about not celebrating the Holy Communion in 'church hours' (that is, when it was being observed in the local parish church). The consequence was that in some areas Methodists still went to their parish churches in the morning. Holy Communion came to be celebrated in the evening, a matter aided after 1804 by the use of gas lighting in chapels and pubs. This style of evening communion following a preaching service continued well into the twentieth century, losing for over a century Wesley's morning celebrations, which had been well attended.

The last of the important provisions was *The Form of Discipline* of 1797, which, while confirming the power of Conference, gave considerable power to local circuits and leaders' meetings, apparently limiting the absolute power of the superintendents. This was to be highly controversial later, when Conference appeared to use its authority to overrule the Leeds circuit leaders and local preachers in 1827.

1796 saw the condemnation of Alexander Kilham. Kilham, when in Aberdeen, poured out a series of pamphlets and manifestos, suggesting greater power for the localities and the laity. Titles such as *Martin Luther*, *Aquilla and Priscilla*, *Paul and Silas*, *Trueman and Freeman* and, most important, *The Progress of Liberty Among the People Called Methodists* (1795) were provocative. He seemed to some like a protégé of Tom Paine, the radical. John Pawson's letters reveal how unpopular he was – 'A. Kilham has produced a detestable book worthy to be burned by the common hangman' was a typical

10. The Plan of Pacification 1795

Part 1 Concerning the Lord's Supper, Baptism etc.

1. The sacrament of the Lord's Supper shall not be administered in any chapel, except the majority of the trustees of that chapel on the one hand, and the majority of stewards and leaders belonging to the chapel (as the best qualified to give the sense of the people) on the other hand, allow of it. Nevertheless, in all cases, the consent of the Conference shall be obtained, before the Lord's Supper be administered . . .

4. The administration of baptism, the burial of the dead and service in church hours shall be determined according to the regulations above mentioned . . . [N.B. Weddings would have to be in the parish church.]

6. The Lord's Supper shall be administered by those *only* who are authorized by the Conference; and at such times and in such measure as the Conference shall appoint.

7. The administration of baptism and the Lord's Supper according to the above regulations is intended only for members of our own society. [N.B. The 'Open Table' is much more recent.]

8. We agree that the Lord's Supper shall be administered among us on Sunday evenings only; except when the majority of the stewards and leaders desire it in church hours; or when it has already been administered in those hours. Nevertheless, it shall never by administered on those Sundays on which it is administered in the parochial church. [N.B. At this time a parish church would have Holy Communion quarterly, or monthly in towns.]

9. The Lord's Supper shall always be administered in England according to the form of the Established Church; but the person who administers shall have full liberty to give out hymns and to use exhortations and extemporary prayer.

10. Whenever Divine Service is performed in England on the Lord's Day in church hours, the officiating preacher shall read either the service of the Established Church, our Venerable father's abridgement or, at least, the lessons appointed by the Calendar. But we recommend the full service or the abridgement. [N.B. This was a source of controversy in chapels for years to come.]

Source: *Minutes of Conference*, 1795. HMGB, vol. 4, pp. 264ff; G. Smith, *History*, vol. 2, pp. 688–94.

comment. For Kilham, power came from below. This was, as yet, unacceptable to the itinerants. By an irony not uncommon in church affairs, most of his proposals were taken on board by the Wesleyan system later in the Victorian age. Kilham overlooked the autocratic character of much of the post-Wesleyan system. He also lacked political acumen.

It has been argued that there was an inherent Enlightenment liberalism in the Methodist system, which would inevitably make itself felt. From responsibility in local societies would stem a natural desire for privileges and rights in church and state alike. The Kilham debates reveal that lay Wesleyanism was creating a more democratic style of church polity than that of the more conservative, and frankly immature, itinerant preachers, and some of the more affluent members who were later to float Jabez Bunting as their representative leader. Even if the New Connexion did not draw many members away from Wesleyanism, it was a sign of great strains within the connexional system.

Kilham's trial at the Conference of 1796 was a foreshadowing of the way in which Conference would deal with dissidents. The result in the first instance was the setting up of the *Methodist New Connexion* (MNC) at Leeds in 1797. There was a loss of three itinerants, including Kilham and William Thom (1751–1811), with about 5,000 members, five per cent of Wesleyan members at a time of expansion. Around Ashton-under-Lyne, in parts of Cheshire, Lancashire and the West Riding – Mount Zion, Halifax is a good example – it proved possible for the MNC to take whole congregations with their buildings. In Sheffield, which was a centre of more radical thinking, 15 out of 22 local preachers joined the new grouping. The MNC never had rapid growth. Its strength lay in the medium sized industrial towns such as Ashton-under-Lyne, Halifax and, later, Dudley. The MNC Conference consisted of ministers and laymen in equal numbers. In the middle of the nineteenth century it endured schism, when the eccentric Joseph Barker (1806–75) became a Unitarian. This divided the MNC at the time when the Wesleyans were in turmoil, suggesting social tensions which were affecting most churches. Later on, an itinerant preacher, William Booth, was not granted the scope for evangelism he desired. He and his wife Catherine were later to found the Salvation Army, which could be called a Methodist-like connexion from the holiness wing, which was surely part of the 'Wesley' heritage. It is ironic that the MNC could not find scope for Booth or for Richard Watson (1781–1833), who became an outstanding Wesleyan leader.

The crisis in Wesleyanism was not over. It was to continue off and on until the 1850s. This is the tension between parts of Wesley's system, which we can call discipline and democracy, connexion and locality, itinerant preachers and lay people. We have seen the solution of the sacramental problem; the ministerial problem was partially solved by seeing Conference as the 'living Wesley'. There was constant tension between Wesley's insistence on discipline and the intensity of the 'religion of the heart', order and ardour. Pawson's wife, Frances, a perceptive lady, was somewhat distressed at the revivalist antics of some preachers in the great Yorkshire revival of the 1790s. Years afterwards, when at Halifax at the time of the Luddite assault on gig mills with some of them facing execution, Jabez Bunting expressed

concern that Methodism was failing in nurture.

In Manchester, William Bramwell (1759–1818) led a group called the 'Band Room Methodists'. Later, his friend James Sigston, a schoolmaster, led a similar group in Leeds dubbed the 'Kirkgate Screamers'. He will emerge again in the Leeds Organ case of 1827. Here he gives an account of Bramwell's later style, which was taken up by James Caughey (1810–91) and others to the dismay of conservative Wesleyans.

---

11. *Revival and nurture 1813*

However solicitous to make the best of this, it is after all an *awful* fact – and it confirms me in my fixed opinion that the progress of Methodism in the West Riding of Yorkshire has been more swift than solid; more extensive than deep; more in the increase of numbers than in the diffusion of that kind of piety, which shines as brightly and operates as visibly at *home* as in the prayer meeting and the crowded love feast. I read of no people professing serious religion who have not as a body far outstripped us in that branch of practical godliness, which consists in the moral management and discipline of children.

Source: W. R. Ward, *Religion and Society in England 1790–1850*, London: Batsford, 1972, p. 86.

---

12. *Revivalism – Bramwell style*

In May 1817 Mr Bramwell had a lovefeast in the chapel at West Moor Colliery. When, after a few had spoken of their Christian experience, he said: 'I am just thinking, there are some penitents here'; and after having united in singing a verse for their encouragement, he commanded all who were determined to forsake their sin and come to Christ, to stand up and show themselves. Instantly there were fifteen or sixteen persons on their feet, all in tears. The first who rose was a stout young man who trembled exceedingly while he cried out 'oh, do pray for me'. Shortly afterwards Mr Bramwell requested all to kneel down; it seemed that every individual was engaged in earnest prayer. In a few minutes the man was set at liberty . . . Mr Bramwell prayed again and several more were made happy. Mr B. then desired the people to sit down. We did so. In a little while, he again requested the remaining penitents to stand up; and this he repeated until there was no one left in unbelief.

Source: J. Sigston, *Memoir of W. Bramwell*, 1839, p. 405; cf. John Kent, *Holding the Fort*, London: Epworth Press, 1978, p. 26.

Bramwell died in 1818, but his methods were later to be seen as typical of revivalism as a technique by Charles Grandison Finney (1792–1875) in America. This was a very different style from that of John Wesley with his reliance on the 'class meeting' as a normal means of enabling those stirred by his preaching to seek lasting discipleship, though charismatic episodes were not uncommon. A more ephemeral style was *Tent Methodism* created by George Pocock and John Pyer. Using a mobile tent, they preached in a revivalist manner. The movement was significant, if short lived.[3] Other revivalist movements did not die away but remained as independent connexions. Some groups like the *Magic Methodists* of Delamere Forest and the *Quaker Methodists*, around Warrington, led by Peter Phillips, came close to apocalyptic groups not uncommon at the time. The *Independent Methodists* (1805), with no paid ministry, brought together the Quaker Methodists and the Band Room Methodists. They still exist, mainly in the north west, now negotiating a Covenant with the Baptists.

In the Potteries, a different style of revivalism was motivated by Lorenzo Dow (1777–1834), an eccentric American, thought by Thomas Coke to be a spy. He certainly combined evangelism with strong Republican sentiments. The Magic Methodists, led by James Crawfoot, 'the old man of the forest', were to be linked with a carpenter, Hugh Bourne (1772–1852), and a converted potter, William Clowes (1780–1851), to initiate Camp Meetings such as the famous one on 31 May 1807 at Mow Cop, a hill on the Cheshire–Staffordshire border. The Wesleyan Conference, fearing government action, forbade such meetings, which were nothing like as long or as undisciplined as some of the American counterparts. They took place on Sundays as a rival to the 'Wakes' and other working-class crowd pullers. *Primitive Methodism*, as it came to be called in 1811, was in the end not so much a schism from Wesleyanism – though Bourne and Clowes were thrown out – as an independent revivalist movement. It had a swift growth down the Trent Valley, across Lincolnshire to East Anglia and Hull, the fishing villages of the north east, the Durham and Northumberland coalfields and Sunderland. Geoffrey Milburn's book in this series must be taken up at this point. It is a fascinating story of a largely working class church in the first generation, not *for* but *of* the poor, taking up an extraordinary amount of the Wesleyan style. A similar movement led by William O'Bryan (1778–1868) in the West Country

led to the *Bible Christian Connexion*. It was as if Wesleyanism could not cope with the freelance style of evangelism of men – and women – who would not easily be disciplined. O'Bryan himself is a notable example of a man for whom evangelism took precedence over discipline and order, unless the order was determined by him. Cornish revivalism was to have a long history producing periodically swift but not always long-lasting bursts of conversions among the Bible Christians and the Wesleyans throughout the nineteenth century.

A serious consequence of the rise of Primitive Methodism, linked with the growth of all kinds of Dissent, was considerable 'media' criticism of Methodism as a dangerous sectarian rival to the Establishment. Several leading writers joined in, including Sydney Smith, Robert Southey (though his life of Wesley was significant), William Cobbett and William Hazlitt, who in a remote country place spots a Methodist congregation.

---

13. *A church for the disadvantaged*

Never was there such a set of scarecrows. Melancholy tailors, consumptive hairdressers, squinting cobblers, women with child or in ague made up of the forlorn hope of the pious cavalcade . . . the pastor of this half-starved flock, we confess came riding after, with a more godly aspect . . . He had in truth lately married a thriving widow and had been pampered with hot suppers to strengthen the flesh and the spirit . . . the jargon and nonsense which are so studiously inculcated in the system are another powerful recommendation of it to the vulgar. It does not impose any tax on the understanding. Its essence is to be unintelligible . . . 'vital Christianity' is no other than an attempt to lower all religion to the level of the capacities of the lowest of the people.

Source: *The Examiner*, 22 October 1815, pp. 684–5; cf. *HMGB*, vol. 4, pp. 351–2.

The war against Napoleon was in full swing. Imaginary scares and old fears of 'Jacobinism' and invasion were still rife. The exemption of licensed preachers from the militia caused the Wesleyan Conference of 1803 to ban the practice of local preachers claiming exemption by taking out licences. In that year the important *Committee of Privileges* was set up, paralleling the Protestant Dissenting Deputies who supported dissenting concerns. An example of what could happen was the case of William Kent in October 1810. Kent, a local preacher, held a service in an uninhabited and unlicensed house. He was fined £20 under the Toleration Act, later quashed by the Court of King's Bench. Lord Sidmouth, who was now Home Secretary, received information from a Justice of the Peace in Stafford stating that fifteen men, nine of them potters, had sought licences while not having congregations. He began to contemplate action. Sidmouth sought to pass a Bill, which would prevent anyone taking out a licence as a preacher or teacher who was under the age of 22, was not appointed to a congregation or could not give testimonials for his fitness for office. Sidmouth presented the Bill in May 1811. He noted that people taking the oaths included 'blacksmiths, cobblers, tailors, chimney sweeps and what not' – carpenters were not mentioned![4]

The debate became furious. At first, Sidmouth appeared to have support from Thomas Coke and Adam Clarke, but the interests of Methodism were better served by Thomas Allan (1774–1845), the Connexional Solicitor, supported by Thomas Thompson MP, who had the ear of Wilberforce. Allan produced from Wesleyanism 520 petitions with 30,000 signatures, while the Dissenters, led by the Unitarian Sir William Smith, produced 700 petitions. The Bill was lost without a division under government pressure. Clearly it would have poleaxed local preaching. The Wesleyans then suggested a Bill, which owed much to Allan, Thompson and Joseph Butterworth, MP for Coventry. It embodied the views of all Dissenters against the Five Mile and Conventicle Acts, which had dogged John Wesley since they restricted the use of unlicensed buildings. On 25 July 1812 the Bill (52 George III c155)

received the Royal assent. Magistrates – a quarter of whom were clergymen – were compelled to administer the oaths to those who sought them, making clear that exemption from military and civic duties could only be claimed by ministers without any other calling than that of schoolmaster. Wesleyanism and the smaller Connexions were now preserved from governmental pressure. The Church of England began to realise that it could no longer rely on governmental support to defend it against sectarianism. The Dissenters were asserting their political clout. Wesleyanism, for the first time, had engaged seriously in national politics. Conference thanked the Committee of Privileges for its work, while affirming its conservatism, exhorting members to 'fear the Lord and the King and meddle not with those that are given to change'.[5] Thomas Allan privately stated his views.

---

14. *Methodism and stability: Thomas Allan*

In times of scarcity and distress, we may safely say that among colliers, miners and mechanics, Methodism has been the grand instrument of preserving subordination and if governments were but acquainted with the happy effects of Methodism both in England and *Ireland* they would do their utmost to protect rather than discourage them . . . we are not a political people. We simply wish to worship God and promote Christianity in the land by all means and have been the steady friends of government.

Source: D. Hempton, *Methodism and Politics in British Society, 1750–1850*, London: Hutchinson, 1984, p. 102.

The French historian Elie Halévy built his famous thesis about the stabilising influence of Methodism and Evangelicalism on sentiments like this, which, later, E. P. Thompson saw as reprehensible. Certainly, popular Evangelicalism could exist outside the Establishment without destabilising it. This was particularly so in Ireland after the United Irishmen Rebellion of 1798 and the Act of Union of 1800.

Thomas Coke initiated an Irish mission aimed at converting the Catholic population from its popery and poverty, the one seen as causing the other. Gideon Ouseley (1762–1839) was seen by some as an 'enthusiast', a fanatic, by others as a second St Patrick. He certainly was an Orangeman. The Methodist anti-Catholic streak, urged on by Allan, must not be underestimated. There was an ominously conservative feel about Wesleyanism, which had to contend with ranters, radicals and revivalists who could rock the boat. An example is the response to the Peterloo Massacre in Manchester in 1819 when the magistracy broke up a demonstration with disastrous casualties and deaths. In Manchester itself 400 members were excluded from Wesleyan societies. The superintendent said: 'they could go to the New Connexion or the Devil'. In 1821, he believed that the change in the trade cycle from the depression of the last few grim years would bring new life to Manchester.

---

15. *Manchester Wesleyans deal with radicals*

The objects we have kept in view are 1st to give the sound part of the society a decided ascendancy. 2. So to put down the opposition as to disable them from doing mischief. 3. So to cure those of them who are worth saving. 4. To take the rest one by one and crush them when they notoriously commit themselves ... They are completely at our mercy ... They are down and we intend to keep them down. That they are not annihilated is rather from want of will than power ... They are growing tired of radicalism and as that dies religion will revive.

Source: W. R. Ward (ed.), *Early Correspondence of Jabez Bunting 1820–1829*, London: Royal Historical Society, 1972, pp. 61–2.

The Superintendent was John Stephens (1772–1841).

Professor W. R. Ward was not off target when he said that the response to Peterloo was to sever official Wesleyanism from urban revivalism. The

---

16. *'Our calling': the Liverpool minutes 1820*

1. We, on this solemn occasion devote ourselves afresh to God; and resolve in humble dependence on His grace to be more than ever attentive to Personal religion and to the Christian Instruction and Government of our own families.

2. Let us endeavour, in our public ministry to preach constantly all those leading and vital Doctrines of the Gospel, which peculiarly distinguished the original Methodist Preachers, whose labours were so signally blessed by the Lord and preach them in our primitive method – evangelically, experimentally, zealously and with great plainness and simplicity; giving to them a decided pre-eminence in *every* sermon and labouring to *apply* them closely, affectionately, and energetically to the conscience of the different classes of our hearers.

3. Let us consecrate ourselves fully and entirely to our proper work, as servants of Christ and His church, giving ourselves 'wholly' to it, both in public and in private, and guarding against all occupations of our time and thought which have no direct connexion with our great calling, and which would injuriously direct our attention from the momentous task of saving souls and taking care of the flock of Christ.

Source: *Minutes of Wesleyan Conference 1820*, HMGB, vol. 4, pp. 367ff.

---

years 1819–20 were the moment of truth for the Wesleyans, as 1792–3 had been for the Church of England. Wesleyanism was never going to be a popular urban religion.[6] It is always unwise, however, to take Manchester as the norm, as later Engels did when he exaggerated the alienation of the working class from religion. William Stephenson, a local preacher at North Shields, protested at Newcastle about Peterloo. His Superintendent urged him to hold his tongue, which he refused to do. Stephenson lost his job as a teacher in a colliery school and was expelled from Wesleyanism. As a consequence fourteen Independent Methodist Societies were founded in the Newcastle area. The price of protection under the law was silence in politics – or rather in radical politics, since a 'no politics' or no partisanship in chapels, except on moral issues, could lead to conservatism.

The Conference of 1820 was in Liverpool. A decrease of nearly 5,000 members was recorded, despite an increase in Ireland. The Conference reasserted the need for 'field preaching', Home Mission activities, prayer meetings and an end of strife with days of fasting and prayer. These resolutions, which came to be known as the *Liverpool Minutes*, were read out at every Conference until 1885.

We end this chapter with a rather different slant. In the 1960s it was the view of some historians that the slave trade was ended, at least by the British, because the merchants and capitalists no longer found it profitable. A Methodist historian, Roger Anstey, suggested that there was a confluence between the Enlightenment and William Wilberforce's concern for religion, justice and humanity. The Evangelical mind accepted much of the moral philosophy of the day, notably the belief in liberty (not necessarily 'democracy') as a cardinal virtue, in benevolence as the duty of men and women, and in happiness as a proper goal.[7] Sadly, the Enlightenment spirit so important to the makers of the American Constitution did not extend to slaves for two generations, splitting American Methodism on the issue. British Methodism was united in following the earlier views of Wesley and the contemporary campaigns of Wilberforce. A modern TV historian, Niall Ferguson, has recently asserted that Wesley and the Evangelical Revival was important for three reasons:

1. The great battle over slavery brought Wesley, and later the Wesleyans, wholly behind William Wilberforce, began a healing of differences between Calvinists and Arminians.

2. A new style of politics was beginning to emerge, of a popular style, which was to lead to the churches activating 'moral crusades' which contined through the nineteenth century.

3. More sinisterly, there was a distinct anti-Roman Catholic style, which also continued throughout the nineteenth century, especially in relation to Ireland.

Two rival Imperialisms were over the horizon.

For discussion

1. How would you estimate the legacy of John Wesley?

2. Would you have supported 'the Connexion' or Alexander Kilham? *Can* we put ourselves back into the past? Do we still need a few mavericks?

3. Should Methodism have split from the Church of England? Could it have done otherwise?

4. 'A church without a head'. Should the Presidency be annual?

5. Has Methodism always been expensive for the poor? Is this still the case in the age of decline?

6. What are the modern equivalents of revivalism? The Pentecostals? The Black Majority churches?

7. What was the relationship between World Mission and the expansion of the British Empire?

Chronology 1791–1820

Wesleyanism		The Wider World	
		1789	The French Revolution
1791	Death of John Wesley The 'Halifax Circular'		
		1792	Baptist Missionary Society
		1793	War with France
1794	Rejection of episcopacy	1794	Thomas Paine, *The Age of Reason*
1795	Plan of Pacification	1795	London Missionary Society
1796	Expulsion of Kilham		
1797	Methodist New Connexion Form of Discipline		
		1798	'United Irishmen' Rebellion
1799	Mission to Ireland	1799	Church Missionary Society
1800	Mission to Wales	1800	Act of Union between England and Ireland
		1800	Napoleon, Emperor of France
1803	Committee of Privileges		
		1804	British and Foreign Bible Society
1805	Independent Methodists	1805	Battle of Trafalgar
1807	Mow Cop Camp Meeting	1807	Slave Trade Abolition
		1808	British and Foreign Schools Society
1811	Sidmouth Bill Primitive Methodism	1811	Missionaries sent to West Africa
		1811	National Society for the Education of the Poor
		1811	Calvinistic Methodist Churches in Wales Luddite Riots in Yorkshire
1812	New Toleration Act Woodhouse Grove School		
		1813	Mission to Ceylon
1814	Tent Methodists begin work		
1815	Bible Christians	1815	Battle of Waterloo Economic depression
1818	Wesleyan Methodist Missionary Society		
		1819	Peterloo Massacre in Manchester
1820	Liverpool Minutes	1820	Death of George III

2
The Era of Jabez Bunting
1820–60

High and Low Methodism

The period after the defeat of Napoleon at Waterloo in 1815 saw economic depression, due to a fall in prices, leading to much poverty and bitterness. In Wesleyanism, the moan of John Pawson, years before, that the Connexion was 'like a body without a head' was heard again. Also there was a conviction that money was going to be an increasing problem with many chapels being built and needing maintenance. Itinerant preachers with families needed adequate manses (a word for ministers' houses borrowed from Scotland) and financial support in retirement. Could rural circuits be maintained? There is an account of what that implied in the early ministry of James Dixon (1788–1871), who became President of Conference in 1841 (see Box 17).

Itinerant preachers in urban areas were becoming more like Dissenting ministers in their lifestyle, although their itinerancy made them still different. The *Liverpool Minutes* of 1820 marked a transition in Wesleyanism to a much more denominational position symbolised by the first Presidency of Jabez Bunting (1779–1858). Bunting's father was a radical Manchester tailor. Jabez studied medicine under the Manchester doctor Thomas Percival, a Unitarian. Entering the Wesleyan itinerancy he was at first on the revivalist wing but was put off by what he felt to be irrational antics. He quickly came to be regarded as an able administrator, becoming the representative figure of those who saw Wesleyanism as standing between the Church of England and Dissent, which was to become the more so when the Oxford Movement in the Church of England began to

---

17. *A rural circuit – Hereford*

Hereford the first circuit to which he was appointed was one of the poorest circuits in Methodism. He covered a vast tract of country, when often lying at great distances from one another, were little places in which a few people gathered to hear the word of God. The Methodist societies were in many parts not regularly formed and consisted without exception of very poor people. The labour and fatigue of visiting this thin and scattered population was immense. Mr Dixon started on long preaching rounds of a month's duration. He walked on foot twenty miles or more almost every day, preached nearly every day and on Sunday walked twenty miles and preached four times. In some places neither food nor bed were offered him. Often he lay in barns and outhouses. Often he purchased some simple food such as warranted no cooking out of his own resources in the villages through which he passed. The circuit was too poor to pay him his nominal stipend and his own little savings were consumed by providing the necessaries of life.

Source: R. W. Dixon, *The Life of James Dixon*, Wesleyan Conference Office, 1874, pp. 27–8.

accentuate high church rejection of the validity of any ordained minister lacking the 'apostolic succession'. Very significantly Bunting had a key role in the creation of the *Wesleyan Methodist Missionary Society* in 1818, with a prototype in Leeds in 1813, when he was stationed there. Overseas mission was now at the heart of much Wesleyan thinking, as was the anti-slavery movement. Bunting and Richard Watson were fervent in support of the *Anti-slavery Society* (1823), which is hardly surprising, when it is realised that of 32,000 Methodist members in the West Indies in 1823, 23,000 were slaves, often persecuted for their faith. In 1825 and 1830 the Conference pronounced on slavery, denouncing it as 'one of the most heinous of our public offences'. United action had been needed on behalf of W. J. Shrewsbury (1795–1856), a Methodist missionary in Barbados. Wesleyans were bidden to vote in Leeds in 1832 – the year when not a few of them received the franchise – for Thomas Babington Macaulay rather than the factory reformer Michael Sadler, who had Wesleyan links.

The thesis of the American historian Bernard Semmel that the Wesleyans siphoned off energy, including the pennies of the poor, into missionary enterprises and indeed imperialism, can be countered by arguing that there was energy for both overseas and home mission. Nevertheless, the Missionary Society became a part of every Methodist's mind-set, for the Wesleyan Missionary Society was different from other missionary societies, because it was under the direct control of Conference with every member of the Methodist Church a member of the Society. What became *Women's Work*, pioneered by Mrs Caroline Wiseman, enabled many women to be involved in sponsoring mission. A visit from the 'missionary' to the local chapel became a feature of Methodist life, continuing until quite recent post-colonial times.

We need to differentiate clearly 'High' and 'Low' Methodism in this period, remembering that the bourgeois Methodists of Manchester were very different from those in Hereford or the tin-miners of Cornwall or the rural Wesleyans of Norfolk who, in some circuits, allowed female local preachers such as Sarah Mallet. High Wesleyanism stressed the connexional, the national and the international stance of the Church. Bunting, more than once, expressed contempt of those who threatened to 'stop the supplies', that is to cease to give to connexional funds in protest at Conference policy. Such, said Bunting, would hinder evangelism in Africa or India. The itinerant preacher was the linchpin of the system, the representative of the Conference. The circuit superintendent had great authority and power, which was, frankly, sometimes unwisely and crudely used. The three-year itinerancy produced a somewhat monotonous style. But it was independent of local power-preventing a 'the parish is my world' mode. This type of Wesleyanism was increasingly conscious of its place in society. High Wesleyanism tended to be conservative, both liturgically – favouring Morning Prayer for instance – and politically. The stereotype of a dominant Toryism and an underlying Liberalism is too rigid. Some more liberal lay people saw Bunting as an innovator. Local studies reveal considerable diversity. There is a distinct air of clericalism about all this, the mark of a Connexion struggling to become a church, but having to attain too quickly the maturity of a national institution. It became easy enough for some local preachers or class leaders to regard the itinerant as no more than a jumped-up layman from the same background as themselves, giving themselves unseemly airs of superiority and priestliness. The theology of high Wesleyanism can be seen as part of a long tradition stated in the 1790s by Joseph Benson and Samuel Bradburn, but articulated much more cogently and theologically by Richard Watson and by the Liverpool-based future Missionary Secretary Dr John Beecham (1787–1856) in his essay *On the Constitution of Wesleyan Methodism* (1839, 3rd ed. 1851) and by Alfred Barrett (1808–75) in *The Ministry and Polity of the Christian Church* (1854).

'Low Methodism' was more local, more lay, more democratic in style, more prone to support revivalism and high-powered 'transatlantic' characteristics

18. *Ministerial authority*

Mr Bunting took the lead in the measures necessary to accomplish the recognition of the itinerant preachers' ministerial character. It had been usual in Quarterly Meetings of local preachers, when the examination of character took place to read all the names on the plan, beginning with the Superintendent. Mr Bunting objected to have his name read on the grounds that it was not the place for any examination of his character, that being done at District Meetings (i.e. what we now call the District Synod) and the Conference. But this means, he drew a distinction between the itinerant and local preachers, which to some extent recognized the proper pastoral *status* of the former. This and other apparently trivial, but significant circumstances prepared the people to regard those who are truly their 'pastors and preachers' as Christian ministers.

Source: George Smith, *History of Wesleyan Methodism*, London, 1864, vol. 3, p. 35.

from Lorenzo Dow to James Caughey, the Irishman from America. It was more consciously dissenting. We shall see later, in relation to Day School Education, when Bunting and John Scott (the first Principal of Westminster College for training teachers) were thought radical! Localism threw up the Sigstons of Leeds, but also more conservative figures like Gilyard Scarth (1780–1853), a master dyer. These reveal class distinctions, which could be divisive. The 'locals' were not necessarily radical in politics, though some of them made high Wesleyans – and indeed Hugh Bourne in Primitive Methodism – shudder. Methodism was now heterogeneous enough to produce all styles of political thinking including those Wesleyans, who were among the 'Tolpuddle Martyrs' who formed an agricultural union at the time of the rural riots led by 'Captain Swing'. The 'martyrs' were persecuted and exiled for using illegal rites of secrecy and initiation. This was during Melbourne's Whig Government. Conference ignored them. Were they not breaking the 'no politics' rule? These two strands have uneasily lived

together in Methodism. There has been no schism since 1849, but many before.

Sociologists often make a distinction between 'locals' and 'cosmopolitans'. The 'locals' are liable to be restricted to home, chapel and work loyalties, while the 'cosmopolitans' were more mobile – socially, spatially and by migration. In the case of Methodists they moved from rural areas to the towns, especially for a time in Wales, and to 'the south' later. In theological thinking, the itinerants, unconsciously, represented a loyalty to a wider church. The alliance between the itinerants and what became the intelligentsia and bourgeoisie of Wesleyanism produced 'cousinhoods' through marriage, which became important as the century moved on.

Nothing typifies 'Low Methodism' more than the vitally important Sunday School movement, increasingly featured by historians. In Bolton on Easter Day 1786, Wesley writes of 550 children taught in the Sunday Schools there. By 1800 there were 100,000 children in the various Sunday Schools in England. This was to become in the nineteenth century a movement involving a large percentage of working class children. It was very much lay-led, producing a significant 'folk culture', though not producing large numbers of church members despite Conference concern over many years, beginning with demands to end the teaching of reading, writing and reckoning on what was increasingly called 'the Sabbath'. This was a matter which in Bolton led to a secession of a chapel and a large body of children, which became the 'Wesleyan Refugees'. Class meetings reached their thousands, but there were a million children in Methodist Sunday Schools by 1900. Historians differ as to their influence – E. P. Thompson seeing them as appalling instruments of suppression, others like T. W. Lacqueur[1] revealing much more working class involvement in teaching. Here was a bridge between folk culture and domestic piety. Its débâcle has never been fully analysed, although Callum Brown's recent *The Death of Christian Britain*, if exaggerated somewhat, points to the vital role which women, as 'angels' and 'mistresses' of the home, exercised in supporting bodies such as the Sunday Schools before the changes in feminine thinking and values in the 1960s. Is this a new version of Halévy's thesis about the role of the churches in producing Victorian stability? Here is an example from Newtown in Wales – my grandfather was one of the children there.

---

19. *Sunday School Festival – Newtown, Powys*

The Wesleyan School was the leading participant in any undenominational Sunday School processions through the town ending with tea parties and sports. In 1872 the *Newtown and Welshpool Express* praised the sight of some hundreds of well-dressed children and young persons parading the streets, in due order and with respectable demeanour. They met in the schoolroom and between 2 and 3 processed, led by the Rev. John Jones, the superintendent minister, along Severn Place over the Long Bridge and to the Crescent where they sang 'Onward, Fellow Teachers Onward'. They then resumed the march, sang the 'Sunday School Army' outside the Bear Hotel [my great grandfather was the ostler there] and 'Our Anniversary Day' before entering the New Market Hall for a bountiful supply of tea, cake (of various descriptions), bread and butter. Trips became a feature in the 1860s when railway building reached Newtown.

Source: Glyn Tegai Hughes, *The First Hundred Years*, Newtown (Powys): Wesley Methodist Church, 2000, pp. 11–12.

In the latter part of the century we hear much of Whitsun Walks, girls' white dresses on Anniversary Sunday (still called 'sermons' Sunday in Lancashire) and tea at the seaside when the railways revolutionised travel for the working class, but in the early days Sunday Schools were subject to gusts of radicalism. Attempts by Conference, led by Bunting, to forbid the teaching of writing on Sundays caused widespread discontent when coupled with Conference regulations of 1823 and 1827 which sought to bring schools firmly under the direction of the ministers. Bunting and his friend Robert Newton

(1780–1854) had sought to ban writing in Sheffield Sunday Schools in 1808.

---

20. *Sunday Schools and writing on Sunday*

Writing is, in all its direct and immediate uses, a secular art. The religious use of it, is at best remote and contingent and indirect. The design of children learning it, and masters in teaching it, is chiefly if they confess the truth, the temporal advantage of it.

Source: M. Batty, *Stages in the Development and Control of Wesleyan Lay Leadership 1791–1878*, London: Methodist Publishing House, 1988, p. 75.

How Bunting thought children at work in the mill could learn is not clear.

In 1827, it was laid down that the Wesleyan Catechism was to be used. Reading or writing could be taught on weekdays. Children were to go to chapel for morning worship. In Leeds, a large body of teachers were ready for a battle with the ministers, who they felt were becoming too dictatorial. In Yorkshire and Lancashire Conference regulations are not always considered sacrosanct! This is part of the background to the *Leeds Organ Controversy*, involving the prestigious Brunswick chapel, opened in 1825. Several factors coalesce. The Sunday School Regulations were one. There was resentment also, as in Liverpool, at the division of a large circuit. The 'organ case' is a notable example, too, of class conflict within Wesleyanism, as an analysis of the Brunswick trustees and the circuit leaders indicate. The circuit leaders were a little lower in the social scale than the trustees. Brunswick was a prime example of large chapels being built for relatively affluent worshippers in urban areas. The trustees of Brunswick voted for the installation of an organ (for which Conference permission was needed) by eight to six, with one neutral. The circuit leaders voted by sixty-to-one against. The local preachers also rejected the need for an organ, thought 'popish'. They were supported at first by the District Meeting.

That should have ended the matter, but there was an appeal to Conference. It overruled the local sentiments. An extraordinary District Meeting, presided over by John Stephens (1772–1841) with Bunting as his adviser, supported the Conference. Bunting said in 1827 'Methodism was as much opposed to democracy as to sin'. He was clearly prepared to 'ditch' the rebels for the sake of order. It was pure Realpolitik. The rebels are little missed, he claimed. James Sigston (1776–1865) of the 'Kirkgate Screamers' and Matthew Johnson, another local preacher, were expelled. The *Protestant Methodists* were set up with an Assembly in 1828. Sigston was its President in 1829 and 1833. The organ had cost £1,000 – and 1,000 members. By 1836, the Protestant Methodists had 4,000 members. The 'organ case' was not really about organs – the Protestant Methodists soon acquired them and even used Morning Prayer in their London chapel. It was a revolt against the power of the pastoral office. The rebels stood for local autonomy, declaring that the 1797 Regulations had been overruled, which was surely the case.[2]

The next important issue was that of Joseph Rayner Stephens (1805–79), son of John Stephens.[3] While at Ashton-under-Lyne, he supported the case for disestablishment of the Church of England. He was told to cease these activities, refused and withdrew from Wesleyanism, supporting Chartism and setting up his own short-lived chapels in the Ashton area. Another issue loomed up. In 1834 Conference decided, at last, that there was need for a 'Theological Institution' to train ministers more effectively. The matter was rushed through Conference, apparently again contrary to the spirit and intention of the Regulations of 1797. Dr Samuel Warren (1781–1862), the Superintendent of the Manchester First Circuit, had been on the Committee formulating plans for new modes of training. The Committee nominated Jabez Bunting, already Secretary of the Missionary Society, to be President of the theological institute at Hoxton. Warren, no mean scholar, and there is a hint of jealousy here, attacked the scheme in *Remarks on the Theological Institution* and was suspended. There was great unpleasantness in Manchester. He appealed to the judiciary, but the Lord Chancellor upheld Conference, a most important judgement. Warren set up the *Grand Central Association*, which sought support for his position, especially in Liverpool. The consequence was the founding of the *Wesleyan Methodist Association* in 1836, which linked with the Protestant Methodists into a new Connexion with free representation in an Assembly and independence for the circuits. In 1857 when they joined the *United Methodist Free Churches* – of which more later – they had 20,000 members, mainly in the north. Warren, who had protested against producing 'cassocked clergymen', left the assembly after presiding over it. Ordained as an Anglican priest, he became Rector of All Souls, Ancoats in Manchester, barely a mile from his previous chapel. Robert Eckett (1797–1862) was the architect of the WMA. He became a minor Bunting, three times President and the President of the UMFC in 1858.[4]

To get a real picture of the group, we need to go to Rochdale. John Bright, the Quaker politician, described the women of that town:

> 2000 women and girls passed through the streets singing hymns – it was a very singular and striking spectacle – approaching the sublime – they are dreadfully hungry – a loaf is devoured with greediness indescribable and if the bread is nearly covered with mud, it is eagerly devoured.[5]

Baillie Street Chapel was the epitome of 'Low Methodism'. Its wealthy laymen wanted to be masters of their industry and their chapel. It is interesting that here – in constrast to Liverpool or Manchester – the poor appear to be left to the Wesleyans. Baillie Street later became a centre of liberal radicalism, with Rochdale pioneering the Co-op.

The idea of a theological college, long ago supported by Dr Adam Clarke, was a move towards a more professional ministry, which was becoming typical of all the churches at this time, as was the case in medicine and education. When the college was set up at Hoxton, to be followed by Didsbury College, Manchester (1842) and Richmond College, London (1843), the Wesleyans insisted that its colleges were connexional, under the control of Conference, not 'party' sponsored as in the Church of England. This had the effect of enabling many different styles of minister to learn from one another, preparing to maintain a connexional style of church and preach a generous orthodoxy. This is still of considerable importance.

New rules were presented to Conference in 1835 concerning controversial issues such as the expulsion of members, meetings for communication with Conference and general matters concerning the life of the chapels. Members expelled could now appeal to the District Meeting and Conference. Memorials were also encouraged from circuits, though they must bear the names of those who voted for them. This sowed seeds, which came to fruition with a spate of anonymous pamphlets in the 1840s. The more liberal element were not appeased – 'too little and too late', said the historian George Smith.

The Hungry Forties and beyond

The 'Hungry Forties' saw extraordinary difficulties in all the British churches. A million Irish people died of starvation. The year 1848 – the Year of Revolutions in Europe – saw the beginning of an economic boom, which stopped some radical movements like Chartism for a decade or so, until the cotton famines of the 1860s. Methodism was torn apart in the years after 1849 showing that although its schisms were internal it was also, to use David Hempton's phrase, a 'lightning conductor' for conflicts still endemic in early industrial England. At this time the Church of Scotland split with Thomas Chalmers leading, in 1843, what became the *Free Church of Scotland*. Its influence on Wesleyans is not to be underestimated. Was Wesleyanism to be the English 'Free Kirk'? Baptists and Congregationalists

had their problems, as did the Methodist New Connexion. Would Wesleyanism have to be the counter to 'high church' Puseyism in the Church of England? High Anglicans were denying the validity of Wesleyan ministry at a time when Wesleyanism was still not behind the dissenting pleas for Disestablishment, as could be seen in the Joseph Rayner Stephens affair. Now Thomas Jackson and others had to respond to 'Puseyism' and the high churchmen in the *Wesleyan Tracts for the Times*.[6]

Wesleyanism was afflicted by controversial pamphlet warfare as vindictive as anything in England since the Marprelate Tracts at the time of Queen Elizabeth I. It was both producing those who revolted against the established order in church and society and disowning them if their activities imperilled the Connexion. Hence the lack of support for the Chartists and the 'Tolpuddle Martyrs'. Now the Connexion appeared threatened again. On one side there were the *Fly Sheets* published anonymously between 1844 and 1849. The *Fly Sheets* expressed dislike of what was called 'Buntingism', with the tendency of some ministers to remain in London leading to its dominance – a constant moan not unknown today – centralization, the power of a

---

21. *The Fly Sheets – No. 4. 1848*

1. We have fixed in the minds of the people generally this point: there shall henceforth be no re-election of the President of the Conference.

2. We have exposed the evils inherent in the modern system of location, centralization and secularization in Methodism.

3. We have proved that there exists a settled purpose of centralising everything in London.

4. We have shown that when a man has wriggled himself into office, he somehow continues to stick there much longer than he is useful to the body, creditable to himself or acceptable to many of his brethren . . .

5. We have shown that the various connexional committees have been formed on the most manifest partiality and exclusiveness. The same names occur everlastingly on the numerous committees.

6. We have shown that those who are for ever

lauding Mr Wesley's plans and proceedings, are as constantly and effectually perverting them by squatting themselves down on one spot for life, carefully avoiding the proper work (in Mr Wesley's opinion) of a Methodist Preacher . . . Methodist Preachers resident in one town for 15, 20 and even 30 years! And these are itinerant! These are the admirers and eulogists of Wesley.

7. We have shown that the cost of the Mission House is excessive, averaging for each secretary £500 per annum . . .

8. We have shown . . . that the grossest partiality has been shown by the dominant party in cases of discipline when the delinquent has been from their own rank.

9. We have shown that in the distribution of office, the same shameless partizan partiality exists.

10. We have shown that the Stationing Committee deserves the appellation we have given it – the slaughter-house of ministerial character.

11. We have shown that the Nomination Committee is a mere instrument in the hands of the Dictator and his tools for carrying their principles out in every department of Methodism. By its means the 'stationmaster' has his men everywhere.

12. We have shown that the preservation of the liberties of the preachers makes the use of the Ballot indispensable in all decisions in which the unbiassed votes of the Conference are of moment.

Source: All the Numbers of the 'Fly Sheets' (1849), pp. 83–5. Abridged. Cf. D. Thompson, *Nonconformity in the Nineteenth Century,* London: Routledge & Kegan Paul, 1972, pp. 134–6.

few connexional 'tyrants' especially the stationing committee, which might send a minister to Cornwall or Cumberland. Dissenters sneered at the 'hundred popes of England's Jesuitry'. *The Times* compared Conference to the Star Chamber of Tudor times. It is generally thought that the eccentric but brilliant James Everett (1784–1872) was the author. If he was not, he must have been green with envy. From the Conference side came *Papers on Wesleyan Matters.* Wesleyan newspapers such as *The Watchman* were full of innuendoes and unpleasantness. How such people could preach on Christian perfection passes

understanding, but the Romantic Age was very prone to exaggeration. Bunting was now long past his period of greatest authority. He had lost some of his ability to spot which way the cat would jump. He was clearly not happy with the style of George Osborn (1809–91) who caused Conference to expel not only Everett but also Samuel Dunn (1797–1882) and William Griffith (1806–83) for denying complicity in the *Fly Sheets* and for their other writings such as the *Wesley Banner.* Far worse was to follow, when superintendents began to expel those who supported the dissidents, as if Wesleyanism was still a very exclusive group. In Derbyshire the Chesterfield circuit had 1,180 members in 1849, 380 by 1851. In Yorkshire Cleckheaton lost 71% of its membership. In Norfolk many Wesleyans left, led by the formidable lawyer and landowner William Cozens-Hardy. It took decades for many Wesleyan chapels in Norfolk to recover.

The consequence was the creation of the *United Methodist Free Churches* in 1857, which scooped up most of the earlier dissident groups including the so-called *Arminian Methodists* in Derbyshire and also some Independent Methodists in Scarborough and Sunderland. It was the first sign of some kind of unity. The UMFC had many of the traditional Methodist features. Allied with that was much more local autonomy. Some of its churches, such as George Street, Burton upon Trent (now Trinity Church), became like congregational pastorates with strong ministers who remained much longer than their Wesleyan counterparts. In Rochdale, the style of Baillie Street Chapel typifies lay control – Sir James Duckworth, the grocer, was President in 1894. A love of revivalism expressed by men like James Caughey, who had a mission in Rochdale in which many claimed to be 'sanctified', was typical. For Wesleyanism the loss of 100,000 members – a quarter of the total – was a 'spiritual earthquake that shook the very foundations, undermined the work of past generations and threatened the whole structure with collapse'. R. F. Wearmouth was not exaggerating. Wesleyanism never recovered its rapid growth, even if it gathered steam again in the 1860s.[7]

It is easy, with hindsight, to castigate Bunting as 'the Pope who never went out of office'. He was a more representative figure than his opponents realised. Certainly he was one of the front-rank religious leaders of the nineteenth century. He masterminded the Missionary Society after the somewhat idealistic incompetence of Thomas Coke. He promoted the election of younger ministers – including himself – to the Legal Hundred and pioneered the right of circuits to memorialise Conference. This gave laymen, often wealthy and rather conservative, a proper place on key committees. He approved the ordination of ministers by the laying-on of hands in 1836. The use of the *Centenary Fund* of 1839 – the centenary was of Wesley's first creation of societies – which amounted to £222,589 showed his priorities: the Theological Institution got £70,000, the Missionary Society £40,000; the rest went to the trustees of chapels, support of aged ministers, Wesleyan

education and the British and Foreign Bible Society.

Although typecast as a 'Tory', he could be called an old fashioned 'Whig', a Methodist Edmund Burke who had much political nous. So he supported the inevitabile Catholic Emancipation in 1829. In the end, he opposed Sir Robert Peel on the grant to the Roman Catholic Seminary at Maynooth in Ireland and Graham's Education Bill of 1843, which supported the Church of England in factory schools at the expense of other churches. After being very conservative on educational matters, he supported Wesleyan day schools in 1847. Certainly Bunting showed inflexibility and insensitivity, while his opponents displayed cantankerousness, which hindered any hope of a genuine partnership between ordained ministers and the laity. Bunting, in the end, saw Wesleyanism as an independent body between Church and Dissent – the English 'Free Kirk'.

---

22. *Professor Sir Owen Chadwick on Jabez Bunting*

He managed Conference because the majority supported his policy; because he formed his mind with rare speed; because he mastered every subject; because he was more moderate in proposals than in manner; because he was a realist; because no one could rival his knowledge and experience; because he bludgeoned opponents with pomposity and rudeness. No one could imagine him young, radical or incompetent. He seemed like a Hercules from the cradle. Across the colonies and the Pacific Islands, from Jamaica to Tonga and Fiji spread the Methodist preachers and missions and Bunting as a Secretary of the Wesleyan Missionary Society financed adventure and directed policy ... a station among the Bantu was given the name Buntingville. A cultured minister composed lyrics on Methodist patriarchs and began in lively anapaests *Great Jabez the Wesleyan Head*. An irritated Mancunian declared with hyperbole 'that the whole Methodist Conference is buttoned up on a single pair of breeches'.

Source: O. Chadwick, *The Victorian Church*, Part I, London: Black, 1966, pp. 374–5.

A wider world

One can imagine that Wesleyanism was becoming obsessed with itself, but a large denomination cannot avoid close contact with government, not only on moral issues like slavery or public order. The 'no politics' rule did not exclude moral issues from the pulpit – but issues of foreign policy came up too. Ireland can rank as such, even after the union of 1801 and Toleration in 1829. Education and the Establishment must now feature.

Two primary problems faced Great Britain. If a nation's constitution is to bear the semblance of a democracy, should all religions be equal before the law? Is Establishment (i.e. a state religion as distinct from bodies tolerated and legally recognised) compatible with equality before the law and with democracy? The Church of England gave up none of its privileges without a fight, sometimes with meanness and venom. The first great battle was in 1828 and 1829, respecting Dissenting and Roman Catholic Emancipation. The 1828 Act repealed the Toleration Act and with it many restrictions against Dissent, though many were still in force such as restrictions on marriage ceremonies which had to be in the parish church; burials in churchyards the conduct of which was restricted to the clergy; Church Rates imposed on all; and admission to the universities. Roman Catholic Emancipation and the admission of Roman Catholics to Parliament was much more controversial. Jabez Bunting, like the Duke of Wellington, saw its inevitability. Outright rebellion was avoided, but many Methodists in England and Ireland, such as Thomas Allan, opposed it, continuing an anti-Catholic stance.

Education is a complex matter, as Wesleyans did not fall into line with other Dissenters. The *National Society for the Education of the Poor in the Principles of the Established Church* (1811), using Bell's monitorial system, had firm Anglican auspices and was by far the largest producer of elementary schools. The *British and Foreign Schools Society* (1808), using the system of the Quaker Joseph Lancaster, taught a simple non-denominational Bible-based faith, which Anglicans could say was pure Dissent. The government gave grants to both societies in 1833. The *National Society*, backed by a more affluent Anglican constituency, outpaced the British Society, claiming £70,000 out of the £100,000 granted, receiving £14,800 in 1848. At their peak, the voluntary schools numbered 14,479 in 1890. Orthodox Dissent divided on the issue. At first, most dissenters advocated 'voluntaryism' which involved a very limited view of the role of the state.

This is what A. V. Dicey called 'legislative quiescence'. It was giving way to a much more interventionist view of the role of the state. Dissenters swung in the end to the view that the state must intervene with either non-denominational education or a secular system, with churches in Sunday Schools performing the role of religious education. This implies a very optimistic view of the churches' strength.

The year 1820 had seen Brougham's proposal for the maintenance of schools from the parish rate rejected with dissenting approval. Dissenters would not tolerate the parson having power, if they could help it. Wesleyans began very carefully in 1833 to support the Voluntary System, but with their own day schools. In 1837, two years before the Committee of the Privy Council for Education was set up, a Wesleyan Education Committee was appointed which presented in 1841 a draft plan for Wesleyan schools which was modified later by John Scott (1792–1868), who was to be a normative influence, particularly concerned for the education of the poor. Under the plan, Wesleyan schools were to use the Authorized Version of the Bible, the Wesleyan Hymn Book and Catechism and be 'avowedly and practically connected as to their government and denomination with Wesleyan Methodism, as a branch of the visible Church of Christ, while avoiding sectarian exclusivism'. This shows a significant shift in a denominational direction.

Clashes came with the Whig Government of 1838–9 over the proposals for a state 'Normal College' for the training of teachers and a much more liberal grant system, which appeared to subsidise other denominations besides the establishment. Dissent, on the whole, was satisfied but Anglicans such as Lord Shaftesbury were furious that it might mean subsidising 'popery'. Bunting made the point that he was against schools being established by the state. The liberal *Leeds Mercury* accused him of inconsistency, demanding rights for Wesleyans but denying them to Roman Catholics.

We cannot ignore the 'Orange' tint of all this,

---

23. *Edward Barries, the Leeds Dissenter, on voluntaryism in 1843*

I am compelled to declare my opinion that it is *not* the province of a government to educate the people ... the proper province of government is to make and administer the laws, to protect person and property and to conduct the external relations of a country; but it is *not* its province to train the minds and morals of the people any more than it is to supply them with food, or to govern their families.

Source: G. Kitson Clark, *The English Inheritance*, London: SCM Press, 1950, p. 135.

which the Irish leader Daniel O'Connell did not miss. The proposal's failure was due as much to the Wesleyans as any other group. 'The Wesleyans ... the Wesleyans must be considered' said Tadpole in Disraeli's novel *Sybil or The Two Nations*. The Wesleyans, urged on by John Scott in 1843, multiplied the building of their own schools, of which there were 900 by 1873 – far more than the Roman Catholics had at that time.

The voluntary system was upheld in the failure of the Bill sponsored by Sir James Graham, Home Secretary in Peel's government, to put through a Factory Act to establish compulsory education for children in certain industries under the clear auspices of the Church of England. Dissenters felt that this was the state interfering in both industry and education. Jabez Bunting, as we have observed, opposed the Bill. His son, William, said of Peel – 'We helped put him in, we must get him out'. Each section of the Christian church must educate its own children, according to a slogan reiterated. Jabez Bunting admitted that the Wesleyans were Nonconformists now (Box 25).

This was the year of the split in the Scottish church, 'What', said Bunting, 'if 200 Anglican priests were to do a "Chalmers" and set up a new anti-Puseyite church?' – or what if they linked with the Wesleyans? The Bill was a gross miscalculation on the part of Peel, bringing the Wesleyans into Dissent. Lord Ashley (Shaftesbury as he became) blamed the 'Puseyites' for pushing the Wesleyans against the Church.

The *Dissenters Chapels Bill* of the next year,

which gave Unitarians much greater freedom, was called a 'vile Bill' by Bunting. The 'Old Whig' opposed Peel again on his proposed grant of £30,000 to the Roman Catholic seminary at Maynooth in Ireland in 1845. Bunting regarded it as ironic that a government should subsidise 'popery', when it did not subsidise a college run by the Established Church.

Ireland always makes it difficult to typecast Wesleyan political alignment. If the *Watchman*, the Conservative newspaper, is to be believed, many Wesleyans supported anti-Catholicism; this attitude emerged again in the *Evangelical Alliance*,[8] of which the Buntings, father and son, were to be honorary secretaries. *Was* Wesleyanism now the 'Free Kirk' of England? If Wesleyanism appeared Tory in the 1820s and 1830s it was still somewhat 'conservative' socially, but not to be relied on by Tory governments. For the Church of England the truth dawned. It was now one denomination among others. It had to use its money and influence in an increasingly pluralist, but not yet secular state. Wesleyanism changed tack dramatically in 1847, a *volte-face* which seemed a betrayal to some Dissenters. The Wesleyans, urged on by Shaftesbury, pushed on with their schools and college building programmes. *Westminster College* for the training of teachers opened in 1851 with John Scott as Principal. It was now prepared to accept direct subsidies from the state, and later to accept the desirability and indeed necessity of a full state system of elementary and secondary education which enabled it to support the Education Act of 1870 setting up Local Board Schools but also maintaining church schools ('faith schools' as we call them now) in a dual system which still exists. All these controversies went on alongside the business of the *Fly Sheets*. Looking back, the education and political controversies may seem far more significant.

Wales, Scotland and Ireland[9]

What of the rest of the British Isles? In Wales, the Calvinistic Methodists (now the Presbyterian Church of Wales), stemming from the work of Howell Harris, were firmly constituted in 1811, dominating the Welsh-speaking work. Wesleyanism (the society in Cardiff went back to 1740), urged on by Dr Thomas Coke, began to consolidate its position in parts of South Wales and in the areas bordering England in central Wales, towns such as Wrexham, Welshpool and Newtown. The great 'watering place' creation of prestigious Methodist chapels in towns such as Llandudno, Colwyn Bay and Conwy was a later development. Wesleyanism was divided into Welsh-speaking and English-speaking constituencies, which are in different Districts to this day. The huge development of industry in South Wales, agricultural depression and the decline of the wool industry led to both population growth in some areas and the Welsh 'diaspora' in the Midlands and the north of England. Wesleyanism in Wales was Liberal in its politics somewhat earlier than in England, and later became increasingly radical.

In Scotland, Methodism tended to develop slowly in the large cities and towns. It had an uneasy history in the first part of the nineteenth century. There was even a move to wind up Wesleyanism there, a matter raised again when the Free Kirk came into existence in 1843. As we have seen, it was a matter of great importance to Jabez Bunting, who saw possible parallels in England. A fascinating development was the work of Dr Adam Clarke in the Shetland Islands. Here was Methodism's greatest scholar proving also to be an outstanding mission thinker and evangelist. Revival, later, came along the Moray coast. Central Halls were set up in Glasgow, Edinburgh and elsewhere as part of the Forward Movement at the end of the century.

Ireland is much more complex. Methodism kept up Wesley's stance of personal concern for Roman Catholic people but with bitter opposition to 'popery' at every turn. Thomas Allan was a leading figure in this after the United Irishmen Rebellion of 1798 and the union with Ireland in 1801. Wesleyanism split over relationship with the Church of Ireland. The *Primitive Wesleyans* (not to be confused with the Primitive Methodists in England) led by Adam Averell (1754–1847) took a stand against total separation from the Established Church. They came back into a united Methodist Church in 1878, after the disestablishment of the Church of Ireland by Gladstone's government in 1869.

The 1840s saw the appalling potato famine with a million deaths and a further million emigrating from Ireland. Methodist membership plunged from 44,000 in 1844 to 26,000 in 1855 due to emigration, both to England and America. Membership increased with revival in 1859. Later in the century a leading Wesleyan was the Irishman William Arthur (1819–1901), who was the first President of Methodist College in Belfast in 1868. In *The Pope, the Kings and the People* (1876), he attacked the ideas of the First Vatican Council of 1870, which had set out the meaning of the 'infallibility' of the Pope. In recent years the college has become a centre of ecumenical work in Ireland, typified by Stanley Worrall (1912–91). The parallel school in Dublin, Wesley College, had as one of its pupils George Bernard Shaw, who spoke scathingly of it. Home Rule came on the Wesleyan agenda later and was largely opposed by Irish Methodists.

Wesleyan strengths

What finally of the strength of Wesleyanism? For those who love statistics the analysis of the 1851

Census of Religious Worship in recent books by Michael Watts and K. D. M. Snell and Paul S. Ell[10] are essential reading, though they do not contain any great surprises. Each reader might like to check the figures for his or her town or rural area or county, comparing it with the latest Methodist figures. It can be a salutary exercise.

Membership was still low in Middlesex, Surrey, Sussex, Essex, Hertfordshire – the so-called 'Methodist desert' – Herefordshire, Worcestershire, Warwickshire, and some parts of the north west. The strength was, claimed Horace Mann, the Director of the Census, in Cornwall, Yorkshire, Bedfordshire, Lincolnshire, Derbyshire, County Durham and Nottinghamshire.

The census showed that 19% of the population attended some form of dissenting chapel on the chosen Sunday in March 1851 and that 13% of the population was in Sunday School with largish numbers of working class children attending. Snell and Ell claim that Church of England Sunday Schools were more open to the poor than the dissenting schools, save for Primitive Methodism. They clearly

had more money. It had always been expensive to be a Dissenter or a Methodist. Nevertheless Wesleyan attendance was claimed to represent 5% of the population of England, showing that congregations included many more than those who claimed membership. Looking at large towns: 12.6% of the population attended Methodist chapels in Nottingham, 8% in Sheffield, 6.8% in Bristol, 6.7% in Lancaster and 5.8% in Bolton. The effect of the 1849 schism must not be ignored when looking at Wesleyan figures.

For discussion

1. Is the idea and practice of Methodism as a Connexion still valid today? Why?

2. What is the role of the ordained ministry? Did Jabez Bunting and Co. demand too much power?

3. Is the local church a democracy? Should it be? Why?

4. What is the role of controversy in church affairs? Should we always seek to avoid splits and divisions?

5. Should the churches have a part in primary or secondary education? Are 'faith schools' divisive or creative? What of *your* area and schools in *your* community?

6. What did Sunday School mean, if anything, to you? Why do you think there has been such a rapid decline?

7. Does Callum Brown's thesis about the vital place of women in church and home seem plausible?

---

26. *Wesleyan Methodist membership in Great Britain*

1801 – 89,259	1871 – 347,090
1811 – 145,614	1881 – 380,956
1821 – 200,074	1891 – 424,220
1831 – 249,119	1901 – 454,982
1841 – 328,792	1911 – 485,535
1850 – 358,277	1921 – 464,945
1851 – 302,209	1931 – 500,010
1861 – 319,782	1932 – 517,551 (Methodist Union)
	Ireland – 30,057

Source: *Minutes of the Wesleyan Conference*, R. Currie, *Methodism Divided*, London: Faber, 1968, p. 87.

Chronology 1820–60

Wesleyanism	The Wider World
1820 Liverpool Minutes	1820 Accession of George IV
	1820 Brougham's Education Bill
1823, 1827 Sunday School Regulations	1823 Catholic Association
	1823 Anti-slavery Society
1827 Leeds Organ Case	
1828 Protestant Methodists	1828 Report of Test Acts
	1829 Catholic Emancipation Act
	1830 Accession of William IV
	1832 Reform Act
	1833 Slave Emancipation Act
1834 J. R. Stephens resigns	1834 Poor Law Amendment Act
1834 Tolpuddle Martyrs	
1834 First Band of Hope	
1835 Case of Dr Warren	1835 Municipal Corporation Act
Wesleyan Association	
Theological Institution	
Rules of Discipline	
	1836 Marriage Act. Civil Marriages
1837 Wesleyan Education Committee	1837 Accession of Queen Victoria
	1838 Anti-Corn Law League
1839 Centenary Fund	
	1841–6 Peel Prime Minister
1842 Didsbury College, Manchester	
1843 Richmond College, London	1843 Free Kirk of Scotland
	1843 Graham's Education Bill
	Maynooth Affair
1845 Wesley College, Dublin	
1844–9 *Fly Sheets*	1846 The Evangelical Alliance
	Irish Famine. Corn Laws Abolished
1847 New Directives for Education	1847 10 Hours Act
	1848 Year of Revolutions in Europe
1849 Expulsion of Everett, Dunn and Griffith	
1849 Local Preachers' Mutual Aid Association	
(LPMA)	
	1850 Catholic Hierarchy restored
1851 Westminster College, London	1851 Religious Census
	1853 Society for the Liberation of the Church
	from State Control
	1854–6 Crimean War
1857 United Methodist Free Churches	1857 Matrimonial Causes Act
1858 Women's Missionary Auxiliary	
1859 Wesleyan Reform Union	1859 Darwin's *Origin of Species*
	1860 *Essays and Reviews*

3

Victorian Values – What was it like to be a Wesleyan?

A divided tradition – holiness

Let us leave the 'Connexion' and politics for a while. There is a deep and fundamental divergence among historians about the nature of Methodism. Is it essentially a holiness group, a leaven within the life of the church? Is the 'grand depositum' of Methodism, as John Wesley put it, really the doctrine and practice of scriptural holiness or was Methodism the re-assertion of religious experience as the key feature of Christian living? Can 'the religion of the heart' be a way of turning the flank of secular attacks on Christianity? Was the historian Herbert Brook Workman (1862–1951), Principal of Westminster College, right when he argued that the doctrine of assurance was Methodism's fundamental contribution to the life and thought of the Church?[1] From assurance, Workman traces Wesley's individualism, his 'Arminian' view of universal salvation and his doctrine of perfect love, which is a corollary of the appeal to experience. 'For if a son is conscious of his relation to his father, there must be the possibility that consciousness shall be complete.'

Recently the American theologian Theodore Runyon[2] has asserted that true assurance must transcend subjectivism. It is not just emotion – 'salvation by feeling', as the Anglican E. B. Pusey put it, but evidence expressing itself in a transformed style of living, in social relationships, in the sacraments, in rational behaviour and always looking to the future, the goal of perfect love. How does that idealistic picture relate to the harsh picture of Methodism given by E. P. Thompson, who sees it as a religious escape from 'social realities'? Did the more revivalist form of Methodism reveal it as a form of Romanticism, which, for many, eclipsed the rationalism of the Enlightenment?

How could such concepts become the norm of a full-scale communion? How could one be holy and preserve the power of religion as a limiting force on the acquisitiveness of human beings? How did this emphasis express itself in the Victorian Age? 'What we can say with certainty . . . is that the conversionist zeal, moral discipline and social concern of countless thousands of evangelicals of all social ranks made early industrial society more stable, more humane and more religious than otherwise it would have been.' Thus David Hempton summarises a mass of historical speculation about the effect of the Methodist revival.[3] Yet the ambiguities of Wesley's doctrine of Christian perfection produced a cleavage of thinking and activity. If justification by faith is followed by the assurance of 'adoption', then cannot sanctification also be ratified experientially? Is perfection primarily an experience as well as an aspiration, followed by growth on earth and then in heaven? This can be a controversial matter even now. William Burt Pope (1822–1903), Wesleyanism's greatest theologian, wriggled on this dilemma.

27. *Christian perfection*

1. 'Pure love reigning alone in the heart and life: this is the whole of Scriptural perfection'. But love is invariably exhibited as the unwearied energy of all good works.

2. That perfection is solely the Spirit's work in the believer; but implies his most strenuous co-operation: as to the former, it is received merely by faith and hence may be given instantaneously, 'in a moment'; as to the latter, 'there is a gradual work, both preceding and following that instant' . . . As employed by the individual Christian concerning himself, it is a term more appropriate to his aspiration than his professed attainment. But this by no means throws doubt upon the possibility of that attainment.

Source: W. B. Pope, *A Higher Catechism of Theology*, London, 1883, pp. 274–5; cf. *A Compendium of Christian Theology*, London, 1880, vol. 3, pp. 28–99.

One firm line would stress *growth* in holiness. This picks up one strand in Wesley's thought, the non-Moravian, 'catholic' emphasis with its roots in the Early Fathers of the Church and Counter Reformation French spirituality. Richard Watson's *Theological Institutes* (1831), though not original, is very important, taking the 'growth' line as did Pope in his *Compendium,* which replaced it for theological students (supposedly!) in the 1880s. John Scott Lidgett (1854–1953) is next in line, featuring filial consciousness of the life of the Spirit, extending holiness to involve political and social life, a matter concerning which Dissenters such as R. W. Dale of Birmingham had criticised Wesley and his followers for being too pious and individualistic. Neither Pope, nor Lidgett, nor even Wesley claimed any personal attainment of 'sanctification', nor did their modern successors such as Newton Flew and W. E. Sangster, who in their various ways sought to exemplify for the twentieth century the central Wesley tradition.

There is another clear line which emerged with Adam Clarke and William Arthur (1819–1901), who picked up and fuelled thinking from the USA. His *Tongue of Fire* (1856) is one of his formative writings; another, *The Successful Merchant* (1852), a bestseller, seeks to show how a resourceful businessman can be both honest and holy – and profitable! This is a very Victorian sentiment. Intriguingly, Arthur seeks what can be called 'a baptism of the Spirit' without 'speaking with tongues' or 'miracles' – possibly a reaction to charismatics of the period. This tradition was then impinged upon by James Caughey, who claimed to 'sanctify' thousands in towns like Rochdale. He was spurned by the Wesleyan hierarchy. Not to be forgotten is the rather different style of Phoebe Palmer (1807–74) from the USA, propounding and preaching a view of 'total consecration' laying one's whole life 'on the altar'. For Palmer, the act of consecration and reception of the blessing of entire sanctification were linked as cause and effect.

Outside Wesleyanism, one can follow Phoebe Palmer's influence on the Church of the Nazarene,

28. *First words of Joyful News 1883*

We begin our task in the spirit of thankfulness. This enterprise comes to the front in a time of peace and increase, and it is our work as it will be our joy to tell of the kindling and spreading of the holy flame of Revival. Why should there not be a spiritual awakening all across the country? And why should not the Methodist people be the widest awake of all . . .

What We Want
News of recent revival. Stories of remarkable conversions. Answers to prayer. Illustrations of providence.

What We Do Not Want
Politics, controversy, connexional finance . . . Buy sixpence worth of this number [it sold for a halfpenny] give it to a hungry boy to sell. He will earn his bread and put good reading into the hands of some who would not have seen our paper.

Source: *Joyful News*, 22 February 1883.

the Pilgrim Holiness Church and (with some differ-ence of emphasis) the Keswick Convention, which still meets each year. She was also a notable influence on the life of Catherine Booth of the Salvation Army, which can be seen as an offshoot of the holiness movement. In Wesleyanism this style was expressed by Thomas Champness (1832–1905), whose work in Bolton and Rochdale was the ancestor of Cliff College in Derbyshire, which celebrated its centenary in 2004 (Box 28).

This style of experienced sanctification and revival-ism, which was more widespread than has been realised, was classically expressed by Thomas Cook (1859–1912), appointed Principal of Cliff College in 1903.

---

29. *The experience of sanctification*

'Regeneration is the beginning of purification. Entire sanctification is the finishing of that work. Entire sanctification removes from the soul all the elements which antagonise the elements of holiness planted in regeneration . . . It is an eradication, the removal of all the roots of bitterness, the needs of sin's disease. We grasp by faith [he cites Agar Beet of Richmond College] the sin-consuming power which sweeps the heart clean at a stroke'. Adam Clarke is brought in to assert 'Believing now, we are pardoned now, believing now, we are cleansed from all sin now.'

Source: Thomas Cook, *New Testament Holiness*, Kelly, 1902, London: Epworth Press, 1948, pp. 29ff.

Cook's argument is not to be dismissed, although I can find no mention of the means of grace or group spirituality so vital for Wesley. This is not so of Samuel Chadwick (1860–1932), who takes up Cook's stance, while more broad in his sympathies, not least in his concern for the poor. He appears to equate the 'baptism of the Spirit' with sanctification, a matter now disputed by Methodist charismatics and New Testament scholars. Can we ask which of these positions is the genuine tradition, or are both the consequences of deep ambiguities in Wesley's

definition of sin as 'the voluntary transgression of a known law', and his sometimes naive interpretation of some of his converts' testimonies? Here is a divergence in Methodist belief and practice which underlies much of its history, not least tensions over worship and liturgy, the authority of the ordained, the polarity of order and ardour, which as we have already seen can split Methodist communities, a matter not unknown today. This description of a Love Feast makes the point.

---

30. *Christmas Day at Hinde Street, London 1842*

On the evening of Christmas Day, a love feast was held at Hinde Street Chapel, at which about 900 people were present. Thirty-four persons spoke with much propriety and power; twenty-five of whom gave a clear and delightful account of the grace of entire sanctification, which they professed to have recently received. When the hour arrived for bringing this interesting meeting to a close, the officiating minister made some remarks on the blessing so frequently alluded to; gave a few plain directions for its attainment, presented to the mind several clear promises; exhorted people at once to seek for it, and then called up two persons to engage in prayer. During the prayer of the first (Mr Thompson) an indescribable awe rested upon the assembly . . . when the second 'Father' Jones pleaded with God an intelli-gent and sober minded young man (Mr James Richard-son) who felt, as he afterwards declared, great objection to excitement and noise in the house of God, cried with a loud voice; 'I have got it, I have got it'. In a moment the whole assembly as if convulsed, such a scene pre-sented itself as cannot be adequately described . . . Every few seconds the affecting cries of penitence were lost among the bursting joy of triumph and faith . . . for ten minutes, this glory filled the temple, during which many obtained the spirit of adoption and not fewer than one hundred persons, according to their subsequent profession received the blessing of entire sanctifica-tion . . . our net increase of numbers taken in March as the result of this gracious visitation is 247.

Source: Robert Young cited in Frank Baker, *Method-ism and the Love Feast*, London: Epworth Press, 1957, pp. 29–30.

The life of ordinary Wesleyans

What happened at local level? Was that Christmas love feast typical? While Wesley greatly stressed holiness, as have some of the most notable of his followers, for most Methodists 'the flight of the eagles' was not possible. Theirs was a 'fluttering of the sparrows' whose holiness was at its best desperate earnestness, at its worst a somewhat self-righteous respectability. Yet it has a style of Christian living which has had considerable influence. Men and women, self-disciplined, self-respecting, self-educated, often enough rather self-absorbed, could not have saved England from revolution, but provided an undergirding to the moral attitudes which were to characterise Victorian England. This could have been crucial later in producing a 'viable class society', to use H. J. Perkin's phrase.[4]

Recently Dr John Kent has shown how Wesley tapped into people's need for 'primary religion', what Wesley himself called 'the religion of the heart'. This changed in a generation into a respectability which meant genuine hard work, moral and financial stability achieved in expanding towns and cities such as Leeds, Liverpool and Manchester or in isolated danger-ridden and hard-drinking mining communities in the south west and the north east and elsewhere, though the styles of Wesleyans could be very varied.[5]

The greatest impact of Wesley and his friar-like preachers was on the group breaking away from the older economic dependency of pre-industrial England. Artisans made their home in Methodism out of all proportion to their numbers in the population. If many of the needy poor were drawn into the movement, they tended to become industrious. They were the folk who became 'labour aristocrats' rather than the totally unskilled labourers or the workers nearly skilled in factory techniques. These social groups produced the leaders of many local Methodist societies in the first two generations and later recruits to the early trade unions who battled for their standards against unskilled immigrants from the countryside or 'Erin's root fed hordes' from Ireland. There is an extraordinary similarity between lists of leaders or trustees in Nidderdale, Halifax, Wolverhampton and the prestigious Hinde Street chapel in London in the next generation.[6] Hinde Street included among its 26 trustees a 'gentleman', a cordwainer, a haberdasher, a Fleet Street bookseller, builders, two tailors, a boot maker, a shoemaker, a cabinet maker, an ironmonger, a cheesemonger, a silver plater, a japanner, a chair maker, a turner and a medicine vendor. The rank and file, clearly, would be somewhat lower in the social scale with, of course, a high proportion of women, a matter which must never be neglected.

Wesley was concerned to communicate the gospel to 'plain people'. Spirituality was to be worked out in small groups which Ronald Knox called 'a theocracy of the petit bourgeois decentralized in a thousand little towns all over England'.[7] Revival without the infrastructure of the 'classes' would be a 'rope of sand', a fact admitted by the great revivalist George Whitefield as well as Wesley. Radical groups later copied 'the class'.

The 'class meeting' is quite crucial to evangelism as well as nurture. Methodism gave those of the artisan groups who were attracted to it a sense of belonging and purpose. It provided a forum not so much for the despair of the workers, as E. P.

---

31. *Nelson's Methodists*

There was a set of fellows called Methodists on board *The Victory*, Lord Nelson's ship, and these men never wanted swearing at. The dogs were the best seamen on board. Every man knew his duty and every man did his duty. They used to meet together and sing hymns and nobody dared to molest them ... these men are the only fellows I ever knew do their duty without swearing and I will do them the justice to say they did it.

Source: *The Methodist Magazine*, October 1808; cited also in M. Edwards, *After Wesley*, London: Epworth Press, 1935, p. 149.

Thompson claimed, but for artisans' hopes and aspirations. Methodism gave people a sense of status when society gave little or nothing. It gave scope for office (for women as well as men), opportunities to exercise talents and a skill in speech and organisation which was often carried over into politics of a liberal or radical kind, even if Conference did not support it. The consequence was men and women of thrift, frugality, reliability and initiative who could move marginally and occasionally much higher up the social scale. Was this a secularisation of Evangelical Arminianism into religious respectability combined with responsibility?

Many of us are interested in family history. Here is mine. My great grandfather was the ostler of the Bear Hotel in Newtown, Powys. His sons became, in my grandfather's case, a harness maker moving from apprenticeship to journeyman status emigrating to Wolverhampton, marrying there a Methodist shoe-maker's daughter. Her father had moved from Sandy in Bedfordshire. Grandfather's brother emigrated to Australia. My grandparents began their Christian life in a small Wesleyan mission but later moved to the circuit church, Darlington Street. My father became office boy to the Town Clerk who sat in the next pew in chapel – grandmother saw to that – and was typical of the Callum Brown thesis about the woman as the mistress of the home. My father had been educated in the Wesleyan School attached to the chapel. He became a senior Local Government Officer and NALGO activist. I was able to go to Cambridge on a state scholarship. This style of social change across four generations must have happened frequently in Wesleyan families.

So the 'sparrows' translated the heights and depths of Christian holiness into what are often misleadingly called 'Victorian values', but were really the values of early nineteenth century artisans. A generation or so later Jack Lawson – Lord Lawson, Labour Party activist – conveys the style well (see Box 32). Here he is in the coal mine.

It is fascinating to see how Wesleyans moved from Wesley's concepts to the 'Age of Mahogany' in the chapels. Rank's Hovis could be made with

---

32. *Nobodies become somebodies*

As we went 'out bye', my pony trotting before, we would talk books while we worked, bent double in the dark roadway. I remember well when this elderly man first struck Nietzsche. That was a find and I also remember how the man turned me upside down mentally, which was all to my good. This man read the New Testament in Greek! Methodism took the 'nobodies' and made the most humble and hopeless 'somebody'. They set aside the things that are not good for a man; they had some little pride in their dress; they made their homes to be things of beauty and aspired and worked to give their children a better life and opportunities than themselves.

Source: Jack Lawson, *A Man's Life*, London, 1932, pp. 111–13.

McDougall's flour with Hartley's jam to spread on it. Reckitt's 'blue' was used to wash with, Mackintosh's toffee to suck, Boot's pills to swallow and papers from W. H. Smith – 'the ruler of the Queen's Navee'. The ships might be built by Morels of Cardiff. Hartley belonged to the Primitive Methodists and Mackintosh to the Methodist New Connexion, showing the same patterns spreading across the Methodist connexions, whose safes in the chapels could be secured with Chubb's locks. Recent work by Geoffrey Milburn and David Jeremy[8] and others has somewhat rehabilitated the provincial Methodist business tycoons with their 'pump priming' munificence; without them, much chapel building and mission would have been impossible.

What were the means used by these homespun theologians of self-help and thrift for the liberation of the poor? (I take it that to liberate the poor is to enable them to become unpoor.) Some of these institutions, such as the *Strangers' Friends Societies*[9] whereby Methodists helped those outside the chapels, were blessed by Wesley himself. In one year in Manchester 1,678 families were relieved with 4,271 visits made. We avoid many pitfalls if we realise that there were working class as well as middle class modes of self-help and self-esteem, of an individual and corporate kind. We need to divide the Victorian period into three – the early period up to the end of the slump in 1848, the middle years often called 'the Age of Equipoise', what economists used to call the age of perfect competition (if you were British); and the period after 1865 of agricultural depression when the 'bitter cry' of the poor was heard, not only in London.

The class meeting tended to become stereotyped in the later nineteenth century. Some people found it a bore, others found its manner of speaking of experiences difficult. But it was defended passionately by educationalists such as Dr James H. Rigg (1821–1909) as the very essence of Methodism. As late as 1928, R. N. Flew claimed that half of the London members of Wesleyan chapels met regularly in 'class'. This is a high claim. Add to it the innumerable leaders – men and women – who visited the members of their class in sickness and in health. That astute lay theologian Dora Greenwell (1821–81), an Anglican poetess, pointed to something crucial.

---

33. *An Anglican view of Wesleyanism*

Philip resumed – 'Do you not think that the secret of the extraordinary hold of Methodism upon the English poor lies in the strict and intimate communion which forms so essential a part of it? Methodism is eminently social; its idea is to journey Zionwards in companies, gathering as they go; husbands, wives, friends, servants, little ones . . . it is the only *real* religion of the working classes; to be "brought in" and to "join a society" is with them synonymous with true earnestness in religion and the conversion of the soul to God. When you are told that such a one is "religious", you always find on inquiring that it means he has joined a society . . . You see what with class meetings and prayer-meetings and preachings, Wesleyans have so much more *means* than church people'.

Source: Dora Greenwell, *Two Friends*, London: Epworth Press 1952, pp. 89ff.

Victorian means of responsibility

The whole life of the chapel, especially in late Victorian times, became a focus for Christian education, partly as a reaction to changes in culture outside, partly as an attempt to combat it. When the Methodists of Grantham built their new chapel, a local poetaster declared:

---

34. *Our chapel*

> Magnificent indeed, it is
> And stately it doth stand . . .
> It stands in Finkin Street
> The centre of the town
> The *Philosophic Institute*
> stands rather lower down.

Source: *WHS Proceedings*, vol. 19, pp. 74–5.

Indeed it did, as Matthew Arnold no doubt observed, although he congratulated the Wesleyans on their day schools when he inspected them. The frugality and the quest for education of that Grantham chapel in the end produced the National Liberal Alderman Roberts, the grocer, whose daughter, now Lady Thatcher, must rank as the most significant of all 'lapsed Methodists'. 'I was brought up to work jolly hard. We were taught to live within our income, that cleanliness is next to godliness. We were taught self-respect, you were taught immense pride in your country. All these are Victorian values.'[10] This was very much the world of middle and late Victorianism when a portrait of *Mr* Gladstone (second only to *Mr* Wesley) stood on many a Wesleyan mantelpiece. Gladstone was the father of Victorian tax policy, of 'peace, retrenchment and reform' as the Liberals put it. Victorian values need careful re-assessment. It also requires a surgeon's skill to distinguish between the various sub-cultures of Evangelicalism and Nonconformity. We cannot, like Sydney Smith, ignore what he called 'the finer shades and nicer discriminations of lunacy'. John Scott Lidgett, describing his home, shows the distinction between the Wesleyans and the harsher styles of some Evangelicals obsessed with pre-millenarianism.

---

35. *A Wesleyan middle class home*

The Methodism of my grandparents and parents was in the true succession of John and Charles Wesley. They were Methodists not Dissenters ... the doctrines in which we were instructed were the doctrines of the Catholic Reformed Church with their Methodist emphasis, interpretation and application ... Deeply religious as they were, they reacted strongly against the narrowness and other-worldliness of the Evangelicalism which at that time prevailed in the Church of England circles of Tunbridge Wells. So evangelical faith and gracious humanity went hand-in-hand in those formative impressions of my earliest years.

Source: J. S. Lidgett, *My Guided Life*, London: Methuen, 1936, pp. 21–3.

If Methodism was the religion of the 'labour aristocracy' and the petit bourgeois, we need to look at interaction between Wesleyanism and society in that stratum of the class structure. The incomes of skilled artisans increased, except for those in domestic industries – croppers, weavers, stockingers and the like – while most remained static until the moderate prosperity of the 1850s, when all began to benefit. Working people developed tools of both protest and revolt, self-help and responsibility.

The first such tool would include food riots and Luddism, when croppers smashed the shearing frames in mills around Halifax and Huddersfield at the end of the Napoleonic wars; and the beginning of the 'revolt of the field' in the Captain Swing riots in 1830. Very few, if any, of the Luddites were Methodists though some were clearly of Methodist parentage. The 'Tolpuddle Martyrs' of 1834 were a different case; several of them were Wesleyans. There was much borrowing of Methodist techniques by the

Chartists with some personal involvement. Primitive Methodists were clearly involved in early mining and agricultural unions as well as Chartism. Self-help was common to all. It is more plebeian and much earlier than Samuel Smiles' famous book of that title, written in Leeds in 1859. The unions were largely limited to skilled artisans, but there was also the great congeries of *Friendly Societies*. There we find the inevitable saddlers and harness makers, hairloom weavers and skilled men from the extractive industries. The *New Poor Law* of 1834 with its principle of 'less eligibility' (greater unpleasantness in the workhouse) was a measure intended to prevent starvation for the poor. It appeared to punish poverty, but in the end became a pointer to welfarism.

So out of discontent, before the social services ideas of Bismarck in Prussia, Lloyd George and later Beveridge, came not only the unions and Chartism, but also the Friendly Societies such as the Independent Order of Oddfellows and the Antediluvian Order of Buffaloes which, at least, assured money from 'the box' in times of illness and a ham tea at

---

36. *Preaching in the workhouse*

There used to be what was called the Workhouse at Wordsley, and preachers on the Stourbridge plan used to conduct services there every Sunday afternoon. The sexes were separated. About 200 men down one side of the Hall and 200 women down the other side with nurses attendant and porters seated at the ends of the rows ... I never had so large a congregation anywhere else. Some had the intelligence of a normal chapel congregation but others could only appreciate something very simple – and perhaps not even that. I cannot say I enjoyed the services or the pitiful sight of many who seemed to think it an honour to shake hands with a 'minister' before proceeding back to their quarters. It makes me thankful that things are so different now.

Source: *Memories of R. E. Lowe* (1898–1990) via Dr Dorothy Graham.

The writer's great aunt was the matron.

your funeral. Here together with the early Co-ops, Mutual Improvement Societies and Building Societies was an artisan's 'masonry' complete with the strange rituals invented by Protestants starved of them in chapel. From an estimated membership of 25,000 in 1815, they grew to four million in 1872, later including 80% of the seven million male industrial workers. Methodists were clearly much involved here. On a smallish scale the *Local Preachers' Mutual Aid Association*[11] was a way in which Methodists sought to help their own poor. In Halifax, Uriah Walker, a magistrate and a Methodist, was embarrassed to have to commit a local preacher to the workhouse. He became one of the pioneers of the LPMA. An annuity of five to eight shillings a week could keep a man out of the workhouse. Here is a prime example of Victorian corporate self-help when there was nothing else. At first the Wesleyan Conference was very chary of the LPMA, since dissidents were involved – a sad reflection of connexional priorities. In 1839 Conference did not allot any money from the Centenary Fund to relieve the distress of local preachers. Associations were set up in Cambridge in 1846 and Bristol in 1849. In July 1849 (the time of the expulsion of Everett, Dunn and Griffith) an inaugural meeting was held. It was followed, in October, by the first constituted meeting, including Holy Communion at Wesley's Chapel. Next year, the first aggregate met – the word Conference would smack too much of Bunting! The Constitution was free of all Conference control, banning controversy on religion and politics – a sad reflection of what internal strife had done. Legitimisation came in the end, for men like Judge Waddy, a prominent local preacher, supported the LPMA and by 1885 the President of the Conference, Frederic Greeves, preached the annual sermon. The LPMA had 10,047 members by the turn of the century with, in 1903, 647 annuitants. This was before the first of the great Welfare State enactments by Lloyd George, granting old age pensions in 1908 and a form of National Insurance in 1911. Since 1949 the LPMA Homes for the Aged have given fine provision for local preachers and their families paralleling the *Methodist Homes*

for the Aged (founded in 1943). All this, wrote Clyde Binfield, is 'the context of chapel, a model of self-control, expressed collectively, offering a life of obedience, discipline, duty and nosiness to individuals in a world where you had only your feet to stand on, there could be no better recipe for stepping heavenwards'.[11]

Two basic styles of self-support and improvement are the Sunday School movement and the *Temperance Movement*.[12] It was, as we have seen, too glib to see Sunday Schools as a means of bourgeois social control. Books such as those of Richard Hoggart have shown how a vague but real folk religion and a vestigial Christianity passed on to several generations of children. This has now completely disappeared and with it the involvement, if marginal, of many working class families.

The Temperance Movement was another instrument of Victorian values. Who will sneer at it now, when alcohol is again a plague as it was in Victorian times? Temperance was not a bourgeois prejudice in its origin, but had more radical and working class roots. Francis Place and William Cobbett saw drunkenness as a lack of self-respect before the 'Preston Seven' began to propagate total abstinence. The Wesleyans were slower than the Primitive Methodists to adopt total abstinence; indeed, they forbade the use of non-alcoholic wine at Holy Communion in 1841, and objected to temperance meetings in their chapels. A small schism in the West Country produced the *Teetotal Methodists* at a time when at Brunswick, Leeds, the preacher would be greeted in the vestry with a glass of sherry. Later Hugh Price Hughes, when a student at Richmond College, thought the teetotallers there a little odd. But soon temperance became part of the Wesleyan mind-set, though it was never an obligation. The 'pledge' could become a secular substitute almost for evangelical conversion, a badge of respectability, still stressed as late as 1947, when I signed the pledge.

Temperance had two effects. One was to widen the cleavage between the 'respectable' and the 'unrespectable' poor, the chapel and the pub. On the main road from Wolverhampton to Sedgley is the Fighting

Cocks Inn with a Methodist chapel opposite, representing two different working class cultures though the pub supporters might well have sent their children to the Sunday School. I would hazard the guess that teetotalism, which the smaller Methodist groups supported early on, was the last nail in the coffin of any Methodist attempt to win the 'unrespectable' poor. The *Band of Hope*, beginning as early as 1834, was a remarkably successful temperance movement with half a million children and young people, providing fun as well as teaching. The fun element is often forgotten in assessing chapel life.

Is it too harsh to say that after 1875, when temperance became normative, the cult of teetotalism and the demands for legislation moving to prohibition was a transition from a religion of faith to a religion of works? To its late nineteenth century advocates, temperance meant prosperous homes. It meant new priorities – better furniture, books and clothes. It might mean healthy and wholesome sports such as cricket and football – Aston Villa began as a club in a Methodist chapel, Villa Road – rather than gambling, contests of brute force or fighting with bulls, cocks and dogs. It was attractive to women also. A tradition of teetotalism had hardened into self-righteousness by the time Hugh Price Hughes was at his prime at the West London Mission. He saw 'the liquor trade' as the greatest of all the existing hindrances to the progress of the gospel in England. Yet temperance could also lead to a more positive view of the state. Legislation *was* needed. If T. H. Green, the Oxford philosopher, was a mentor behind radical liberation, it needs to be remembered that his aim of 'removing hindrances to freedom' could be seen to include not only legislation against the drink trade and the 'beerage' but in the end the beginning of the Welfare State. Hughes even said that Green's lectures were 'the philosophical expression of the grand old Methodist doctrine of entire sanctification'. Green might not have been flattered, but Hughes was pushing the old Wesleyan doctrine into the stance taken up by John Scott Lidgett, when he led the Progressives on the London County Council.

This was the religious frontier of the 'labour aristocracy', the world of the chapel, the smell of which Robert Browning so disliked, the lack of that 'sweetness and light' which Matthew Arnold so patronisingly and unfairly despised. Most Methodists were of this class – but not all. Go to Darlington Street Chapel in Wolverhampton in 1848 when the town became a borough. In the gallery over the clock – the top seats – would sit the ironmaster G. B. Thorneycroft, the first Mayor, and his friends who were to dominate the town's politics. Thorneycrofts, Hartleys, Fowlers were names to conjure with in West Midlands Wesleyanism. Fowler became the first Methodist peer and the first Wesleyan Cabinet Minister when vainglory would boast of such. Towns such as Bolton and Halifax had chapels called 'Mayor's Nests' because many self-made entrepreneurs and mill-owners dominated local government with patriarchal concern for the town and, after 'the dark satanic mills' era, for their employees. Sir Isaac Holden (1807–97), the Wesleyan in Bradford, might not have been as mighty as Sir Titus Salt, the Congregationalist creator of Saltaire, but he was a powerful force in the West Riding of his day, preferring revival to liturgy. These were provincial Methodists of enterprise and homely paternalism who influenced chapel and municipality alike. No doubt, some would see efficient business as not a proper sphere for the Christian – Matthew Arnold might lift his cultural skirt at it, but Wesleyanism, at this time, was a provincial faith and did not – could not – sneer at business.

Was it all suffocating to culture? 'We don't live in the days of the Barons, thank God,' said the politician Brougham in 1821, 'we live in the days of Leeds and Bradford and Halifax and Huddersfield' – was it all muck and mills and Methodism? It was also part of the world of Romanticism. Mendelssohn was sung along with Handel's *Messiah* at the Halifax and Huddersfield Choral Societies (packed with chapel folk) and John Foster's Black Dyke Mills Band was just up the hill at Queensbury. The brass band and the chapels declined together!

37. *What I owe to the Chapel. Fernhead Road, Paddington.*

I owe a special debt to the old chapel. It was there in the Bible class and Guild I was encouraged to speak. It started by reciting at an early age and later to read the lesson in church on Anniversary Day. I think the early experience gave me some degree of immunity from nervousness on a public platform. I was never taught elocution, but critics in the family circle were severe enough then as they are now to impress upon me the essentials which I believe to be clarity in articulation and the necessity of controlling the voice as to ensure that the most distant member of an audience can hear distinctly without feeling he is being shouted at. The old chapel attracted in those days a great company of youth, some of whom possessed a mental equipment much above the average. Some of them won distinction in the Civil Service, the professions and business.

Source: Harold Bellman, *A Cornish Cockney: Reminiscences and Reflections*, London: Hutchinson, 1947, pp. 40–1.

Robert Moore[13] was not far off the mark when he characterised a Methodist of the Deerness Valley in County Durham as a 'highly disciplined, self-controlled person, willing to train his mind, and his voice in harmony singing'. In the chapels a non-drinking, non-gambling social centre provided almost the only legitimate sources of entertainment for women. From the chapels there poured out into the new professions and bureaucracies of a buoyant economy of Britain and the Empire thousands of men and women of integrity and earnestness. There was, too, the woman primary school teacher – an influence on British life of immense importance. Many of them were Methodists – out of all proportion to the size of the Wesleyan church. The dedication of the growing caring professions owed much to the lesser, unsung Florence Nightingales of Methodism.

There was another world too. Samuel Drew (1765–1833) of St Austell, a local preacher, was called the 'Methodist Plato' and was worthy of a London chair of philosophy; James Smetham (1821–89) was trying to combine Pre-Raphaelite art and Methodism; John Couch Adams (1819–92), Professor of Astronomy at Cambridge, showed a new area where Methodists were beginning to infiltrate. There were fascinating Wesleyan 'cousinhoods' in the late Victorian era – the Osborns, Gregorys, Derrys, Moultons, MacDonalds. George MacDonald (1805–68) – minister at Hinde Street, London and Trinity Wolverhampton – is one of the few Methodists to creep into A. N. Wilson's recent tour de force *The Victorians*. One daughter of Hannah and George MacDonald married Alfred Baldwin, the Bewdley iron-master – their son was Stanley Baldwin, Prime Minister. Another was the mother of Rudyard Kipling, a third married the artist Sir Edward Burne-Jones, a fourth married Sir Edward J. Poynter, and the youngest sister was housekeeper for the Baldwins. Fred, their brother, was a tutor at Handsworth College, Birmingham and later Secretary of the

38. *Essential Wesleyanism 1913*

With us the emphasis is still on the doctrine of conversion ... we would be forced to drop the name of Wesley if we were unfaithful to that ideal ... Then there comes the doctrine of experience that for every man the greatest of all reasons for believing is his own power to say: 'Once I was blind, but now I see'. With it stands the doctrine of holiness – the declaration that nothing less than perfect love of God and man can ever satisfy God's claim upon us, and that by his indwelling Spirit men can and must press on towards that perfection here, and not wait for it beyond the grave. These were the great doctrines that Wesley rediscovered; and it is on the strength of our unwavering hold on them that we remain Wesleyans today.

Source: J. H. Moulton, *A Neglected Sacrament*, London: Epworth Press, 1919, pp. 20–1.

J. H. Moulton was killed by submarine action in 1917, returning from India.

Missionary Society and President of the Conference
in 1899. There is something hard to define but distinctly Wesleyan about the Moultons, the missionary
factor coming into it clearly with consecrated
scholarship which, after all, is the heart of holiness.
The Moultons nevertheless supported wholeheart-
edly Moody and Sankey and were influenced by them
as were many such as R. W. Dale and George Adam
Smith, the redoubtable Scottish biblical scholar.
James Hope Moulton, while Professor at Manchester, wrote about Zoroastrianism, acknowledging
the spiritual reality of other religions, but he could
still point to the heart of Methodism (Box 38).

This takes us to where we began this chapter. The
Congregationalist R. W. Dale, who claimed that the
class meeting was the most original and striking of
all the fruits of the revival, also claimed that the
doctrine of Christian perfection was where Wesley
left it. I hope we have shown that this was not really
the case. It was a much more complicated story than
that.

For discussion

1. What can 'sanctification' mean to an ordinary
   member of a Methodist congregation?

2. Does Methodism have a particular appeal to
   some people? Who? Why?

3. Did 'teetotalism' put many working class people
   off Methodism?

4. Why did Methodism tend to become middle
   class? Look at your church's demography and
   your family history.

5. Why did the last generation so denigrate
   Victorian businessmen and Victorian values?

6. Ought we to be much more concerned about
   local government?

4

Wesleyan Worship

Service books and styles

What of worship in Wesleyanism? If the phrase 'There are many Methodisms' is tiresome, it is certainly true of worship. Wesleyanism stood between the Church of England and Protestant Dissent, not least in styles of worship. It influenced and was influenced by both. If one attended Wesley's Chapel in London the service in the morning would be Morning Prayer, according to the Book of Common Prayer of 1662 or Wesley's abridgement of it in his *Sunday Service*. Most large towns had at least one chapel, where this was the norm throughout the nineteenth century. Typical were Park Street, Bolton, St John's, Sunderland, or Trinity, Wolverhampton, where H. H. Fowler (later Lord Wolverhampton) was dominant. He insisted on its use from the opening of the chapel. This was still the norm there in the 1950s. It is strange that there were radical Methodists who thought all this a 'High Methodist' innovation. It was a continuance of Wesley's tradition, although Jabez Bunting did introduce it at the opening of the Conference, a custom maintained until the 1970s. The opinion of Adam Clarke, scholar and evangelist, is recorded (Box 39).

It is the case that leaders of Methodism such as Clarke and Thomas Jackson maintained for a generation that the most edifying type of worship for Wesleyans was a union of the formal and the free, using Christian tradition and the guidance of the Holy Spirit. Evening worship – the maids could attend – helped by the growing use of gas lighting –

saw a much freer form used than Morning Prayer.

Holy Communion, after 1795, normally took the form laid down in the *Book of Common Prayer*, or the Sunday Service[1] and its reprints, although it is clear that it was often abbreviated. It nearly always followed an evening preaching service with the bread

---

39. *Morning Prayer – a plea for its use*

With respect to the introduction of the Liturgy of the Church of England – this book I reverence next to the Book of God. Next to the Bible, it has been the depository of the pure religion of Christ; and had it not been laid up there, and established by Act of Parliament, I fear that religion would, long ere this have been driven to the wilderness. Most devoutly do I wish that whenever we have service on the Lord's Day, we may have the prayers read. This service contains that form of sound words to which in succeeding ages an appeal may be successfully made for the establishment of the truth professed by preceding generations. Had it not been under God for this blessed book, the Liturgy of the English Church, I verily believe Methodism had never existed. I see plainly that where we read these prayers, our congregations become better settled, better edified and put further out of the reach of false doctrine. Introduce the Church Service in God's name not in any *Abridgement* but in the genuine original.

Source: T. P. Bunting, *The Life of Jabez Bunting*, Woolmer, 1887, p. 358.

(This was advice by Adam Clarke to Joseph Entwistle about the Liturgy at Brunswick Chapel, Liverpool.)

and wine normally received only by the members. It is estimated that congregations consisted often of three times as many 'adherents' as members, so the numbers at Holy Communion tended to be much smaller than those who were present at the preaching service. The adherents would leave at a 'break' between the preaching service and Holy Communion. The congregation would go up to the table in groups, a distinctive Wesleyan practice which still persists, greatly valued by some as a corporate act, though its origin is probably eighteenth century Anglicanism. A chalice would be used to administer the wine. The temperance lobby, later in the century, insisted on the use of unfermented wine, although it had been forbidden by the Conference in 1841. Germ conscious Edwardians introduced the small glasses, which became the norm across the Free churches, chalices being hidden away in cupboards until recent times. There is no evidence of greater Anglican propensity to infection, but the use of alcohol may have an antiseptic quality. In recent times the Table of the Lord has been 'open' to all the baptised and to members of other Christian churches but as late as 1923 it was asserted: 'that the Table of the Lord shall be open to all comers is surely a great discredit and a serious peril to any Church'. This is an example of a Conference statement that came to be largely ignored in the chapels.

In 1882, a new Wesleyan service book was published and widely used, until the *Book of Offices* of 1936, after Methodist union. This book was deeply influenced by J. H. Rigg and Dr Benjamin Gregory (1820–1900). It eliminated any possible suggestion of the baptismal regeneration of infants, even if Wesley believed it. In the Communion Service, the Cranmerian 'prayer of consecration' was slightly watered down and the 'Manual Acts' of breaking bread and raising the cup were omitted, making the liturgy rather cerebral, lacking in visible ceremony. The manual acts do not officially appear until the *Sunday Service of 1975*. In Wesleyanism only ministers received into Full Connexion could preside at Holy Communion, until probationers began to do so, with Conference permission, in cases of necessity.

This was at the end of the nineteenth century. It was a concession not overlooked when negotiations took place with the United Methodists and Primitive Methodists, who wished lay presidency to be preserved, a pointer to what was called the priesthood of all believers, interpreted to exclude ministerial monopoly of presiding at Holy Communion.

It must be remembered that many Wesleyans still attended the parish church throughout the nineteenth century. In Bradford, for instance, for a time they went en masse to the church presided over by the popular John Crosse. Wesleyans continued to look to the parish church for baptisms and other rites of passage. Until the Marriage Act of 1836, marriages were only possible in the parish church. After the Act the Registrar could be present at marriage ceremonies in a chapel if it was registered. Not until 1898 was it possible for Free Church ministers to act as 'authorised persons' in their chapels. Wesleyans in Parliament – H. H. Fowler and R. W. Perks – led moves to persuade the government to enable Free Church ministers to conduct funerals in parish churchyards. This was allowed after 1880 by Osborne Morgan's Burial Law Amendment Act, with further clarification in 1900. This has been called the last major political victory of militant Dissent in England. In 1841, the Vicar of Gedney, T. S. Escott, refused to bury a child who had been baptised by a Wesleyan minister, calling the itinerant preachers 'beings who pretend to be ministers of the Gospel and really are ministers of Hell and dissenting mountebanks'. In the end the Court of Arches ruled that baptism by Wesleyan ministers was valid by canon and civil law. Escott appealed to the Privy Council who upheld the Court of Arches.[2] A negative verdict would have made any baptisms in Methodist chapels difficult to sustain. Certainly the decision had the effect of increasing dissenting feelings in Wesleyanism. Many Methodist chapels in the north had their own churchyards, which avoided this kind of appalling assumption of pompous superiority. But the matter of Anglican allegiance was complex. In Wolverhampton, ironmaster Thorneycroft and his friends, whom we have mentioned, would worship at St Peter's, the parish church, in the morning and 'chapel' in the evening.

In 1839 George Wilkins, Archdeacon of Nottingham, wrote to his bishop asking advice on what to do with candidates presenting themselves for confirmation who also attended dissenting, probably Wesleyan, places of worship. Only as late as 1894 did the Wesleyans issue a service for the Recognition of Church Membership, which gave a style, which came to be officially called Confirmation in the 1960s. This was another 'marker', which made Wesleyanism a 'church' rather than a 'society'. While the description of some Wesleyans as a 'band of denominational gypsies of no fixed abode' may be an exaggeration, there is no doubt that many would not find it odd to hear that on 5 February 1804 Richard Robarts, a Cornish local preacher, made a typical entry in his diary: 'Sunday, a good day in general; I found profit in church and sacrament. In the evening, according to my plan I preached for the first time at home, Trispian.' Frances Knight shows that this was not uncommon but, as we shall see, the hardening of Anglican attitudes was a factor in making flitting between 'church' and 'chapel' more rare as the century wore on.

What of the 'preaching service'? Thomas Jackson, later President and Wesleyan patriarch and editor of Wesley's works, describes worship as he experienced it in his youth at Pocklington, in Yorkshire (Box 40).

Preaching services, love feasts and other 'prudential means of grace', as Wesley called them, grew in popularity and were increasingly open to a wider public than 'society' members in the days of Bunting's youth when he was rebuked for attending a love feast without a class ticket. This increasingly – especially when large chapels were built – gave the preaching service the feel of an open air service with a roof on – and a service for evangelism as well as for edification leading to the kind of style at the West London Mission at the beginning of the twentieth century. Mark Guy Pearse (1842–1930) would preach to 'the saints' in the morning with a liturgical service, while Hugh Price Hughes having let fly on politics in the afternoon 'Conference' as he called it,

---

40. *A preaching service*

In the Pocklington circuit at the time there were few chapels; so that our meetings for preaching and public worship were mostly held in the kitchens of farmhouses and the cottages of labouring men. The preacher usually stood behind a chair the back of which supported a moveable desk upon which lay his bible and hymn-book, the people standing or sitting upon chairs, tables, stools or chests of drawers, as the case might be. In these humble sanctuaries, the people worshipped God in spirit and truth, as their entire behaviour indicates. The sermons to which they listened contained no elaborate phraseology, no disquisitions on dark and doubtful questions and no hard technical terms; their substance being the essential truth of Christ's gospel, and their garb pure Saxon English which even the children could understand, delivered with a broad Yorkshire accent. The sentiments embodied in the hymns that were sung, and in the prayers that were offered the people felt in their own hearts. There was nothing artificial in their service . . . at lovefeasts many a tale of personal conversion was told and listened to, with tears of grateful joy.

Source: Thomas Jackson, *Recollections of My Own Life and Times*, London, 1873, pp. 64–5.

---

would preach an evangelistic sermon in the evening expecting converts.

In 1815 Jonathan Crowther[3] set out a typical order of service – Hymn, Prayer, Hymn (few verses), text, sermon, Hymn, Prayer, Benediction – 'plain, simple and edifying', showing that Joseph Nightingale's critical survey of 1807 (Box 41) was accurate.

Scripture reading was, as Nightingale implies, not always included, though it became normal by 1820. The basic units clearly were extempore prayer, extempore though not unprepared preaching, and the singing of hymns, at first 'lined out' by the preacher. As most congregations became literate, a significant factor, Methodists began the custom of taking their own hymnbooks to worship with them. This created a very important 'oral' tradition of

The mode of conducting divine worship among the Methodists is of all others the most regular and simple. If their plan is defective in any point, it is in not having the Scriptures read to the people ... public worship is begun by singing the hymns being given out line by line by the preacher. After singing follows prayer; then singing again; to which succeeds an extempore sermon; after this yet another hymn is sung; and then the service is finally concluded by prayer and the customary benediction. The whole service usually lasts about an hour in the morning; at noon and, in the evening about an hour and a half. This however depends much upon the prudence, the zeal and the modesty of loquacity of the preachers. I have known the congregation kept in pain for two hours. The service of the Wesleyans is, however upon the whole shorter and more simple than that of the Whitefieldians or Calvinists whose preachers are usually extremely tiresome.

Source: Joseph Nightingale, *A Portraiture of Methodism*, London, 1807, pp. 252ff.

Forth in thy name, O Lord, I go,
    My daily labour to pursue,
Thee, only thee, resolved to know
    In all I think or speak, or do.   HP 381

The influence of Charles Wesley must not be underestimated in the pattern of Wesleyan worship. The 1780 Collection was in general use. In 1800 a supplement was added with the number of hymns rising from 525 to 560, including seven hymns on the Lord's Supper. In 1831, a further supplement was prepared by Richard Watson, Thomas Jackson and Jabez Bunting. This brought the total to 769 of which 668 were by the Wesleys. In 1877 another supplement contained 1,026 hymns and metrical psalms and was in general use until 1904 when the *Methodist Hymn Book* followed the style laid down by *Hymns Ancient and Modern* in 1861. The set out of the Christian year and elements of Christian doctrine and life ended the style of the 1780 Collection. During the century there were also official books for Sunday School and day school use. If John Wesley wanted only 'our hymns' to be sung for doctrinal reasons, he was wise, but congregations would often 'do their own thing' with the use of revivalist hymns as in Primitive Methodism, with, later in the century, the hymns which came to be called 'Sankeys' – the famous *Hymns and Sacred Solos*. These were followed by choruses stemming from Cliff College. So the hymnody, particularly outside Sunday worship, was more varied than Conference might have wished. Jabez Bunting was

hymnody, which was of great importance in passing on Evangelical Arminianism through remembered words, a way almost unique in Christendom. The hymnbook was used together with the Bible in private devotion. I possess my Welsh grandfather's hymnbook, black with use in his simple evening devotions. His extempore prayers were largely remembered hymn verses and psalmody. When 'lining-out' had ceased, the service would be filled out with more hymns and later still in the large town chapels with introits, anthems, canticles like the Te Deum and also Psalms, with organs and choirs to lead the congregation.

So, by the early twentieth century, the service could be, even when Morning Prayer was not used, quite elaborate with hymns becoming very much 'our liturgy' rather than just filling gaps as could be the case in Anglican worship. Each hymn, if the preacher was wise, articulated a part of worship – praise, confession, a prologue to the sermon, a follow-up to the sermon and a final act of dedication –

42. *A Victorian preaching service*

1. Introit. 2. Collect. 3. Hymn. 4. Prayer. 5. Chant. 6. First lesson. 7. Chant. 8. Second lesson. 9. Hymn. 10. Sermon. 11. Anthem. 12. Hymn. 13. Benediction.

Source: Wesleyan Chapel, Eccles, *Service Book*, 1884. The 1891 edition stated: 'The Hymns or such portions as the minister may indicate are sung through without a break from the Psalter and the order of service'.

put off by revivalist music, but it will be no surprise to Yorkshire, Lancashire or Cornish readers that its use was common. It is significant that after the eighteenth century Wesleyan hymn writers were few – W. M. Bunting was one but forgotten now – such was the dominance of Charles Wesley. Welsh speaking congregations were the exception with William Williams Pantycelyn dominant in the Welsh hymn books.[4] In England, he is known as the author of 'Guide Me O Thou Great Jehovah'. We end this section with William Arthur, the notable Irish writer, pointing out the two traditions which ran together in his tradition of Wesleyanism.

---

43. *Form and spontaneity 1856*

He who will never use a form in public prayer casts away the wisdom of the past. He who will use only forms casts away the hope of utterance to be given by the Spirit at present and even shuts up the future in the stiff hand of the past ... to object to all forms is narrowness. To doom a Christian temple to be a place wherein a simple and impromptu cry may never rise to heaven is superstition.

Source: William Arthur, *The Tongue of Fire*, London, 1856, pp. 20-1.

The preachers, chapels – and signs of new life

What of the great tradition of preaching? Wesley pleaded for 'plain truth for plain people'. The greater preachers after his day included Samuel Bradburn, 'the Methodist Demosthenes', Richard Watson with his passionate vision of world missions, and the remarkable scholar-evangelist Adam Clarke. Jabez Bunting clearly began as a preacher – his printed sermon on justification by faith is notable – but his work as church organisation man seems to have taken the edge off his style. The popular preacher of the mid-Victorian period was Robert Newton who became well known on the coach and railway system. In fact the 'railway mania' produced popular preachers who opened innumerable chapels and preached about world mission too. Newton would repeat himself countless times, which was always a danger of Methodist preaching! This did mean both professional skill but also sometimes artificiality, but Newton had the skill of immediately grabbing a congregation's attention and holding it. A later popular figure was William Morley Punshon (1824–81). He preached and lectured on Bunyan, Wilberforce and the Huguenots with the intention of raising money for the 'Watering Places Fund' – Methodism was moving to Bournemouth! – and the Metropolitan Chapel Fund. He turns up at Newtown in 1878 to give his lecture on the Mayflower, which could be cleverly geared to current political events. Here he is at Exeter Hall:

---

44. *Punshon stirs them up*

He spoke with immense energy and force ... Feeling among the audience grew, enthusiasm was awakened and gathered force as he went on. At last, in one of the magnificent climaxes, the vast congregation sprang simultaneously to their feet. Hats and handkerchiefs were waved, sticks and umbrellas were used in frantic pounding of the floor ... such a tornado of applause swept through Exeter Hall and swelled from floor to ceiling as I have never witnessed before or since.

Source: Gordon Rupp, 'The influence of Victorian non conformity' in *The Listener* 17 March 1955, p. 470.

This was a style of Romanticism very different from Bunting or Adam Clarke.[5]

Most Methodist services, particularly in the small rural chapels, were conducted by local preachers who sometimes felt 'dumbed down' by the ministers who monopolised the 'big pulpits', increasingly accused of leaving rural chapels to look after themselves. This annoyed some local preachers such as Judge Samuel Waddy (1830–1902) who felt that ministers were becoming too pompous and priestly.[6] Local preachers were very varied indeed in their social class and styles, becoming more professional as the century wore on. By the twentieth century, in some areas, the teaching profession was becoming dominant. Here is a nineteenth century description.

---

45. *Village Methodism – the local preacher*

James Barnett . . . is classified as a shoemaker and he did indeed make shoes as well as mend them. Girls used to complain that his shoes of heavy utility types made for hard wear, never wore out.

He lived at Pilton in one of the two thatched cottages later amalgamated to form Taylor's farmhouse and an apple tree he planted in the garden still flourishes. On Sunday he conducted services in Methodist chapels in the Salisbury circuit and had a reputation as a notable preacher. His working day began at four o'clock in the morning and by rota each of his four daughters had to rise with him and read the Bible for four hours till breakfast at eight o'clock. Those who knew him said he was a dear old man but that his wife was a bit of a dragon. A surviving Salisbury circuit plan records James Barnett's preaching appointments for the quarter from November 1874 to February 1875. They were at chapels at Winterslow, Idmiston, West Dean, Pilton (his home church), Broughton, Winterbourn, Farley and West Grinstead. In each case he expected to conduct two services, one in the morning and one in the evening, someone in the village supplying hospitality. Most appointments involved a journey of from two to four miles each way. The journey home in this quarter was inevitably in darkness. He was, of course, only one of thousands of local preachers with such a Sunday schedule before the age of the motor car.

Source: Ralph Whitlock, *A Victorian Village*, London: Robert Hale, 1990, p. 195.

We can compare Thomas Thompson (1754–1828), MP, friend of Wilberforce, first lay treasurer of the Wesleyan Methodist Missionary Society with William (Billy) Dawson (1733–1841) working in Yorkshire. Preaching at Brunswick, Leeds, he was annoyed to find a notice stating 'the trustees wishing to accommodate the respectable friends who may attend on this occasion propose to reserve the entire gallery of the Brunswick chapel for their use. To facilitate this, silver will be taken at the foot of the stairs'. Perhaps only Methodism could make use of Sammy Hick (1779–1849), the Aberford blacksmith, who preached throughout Lancashire and Yorkshire offering a gospel of holiness, and indeed miracles, in a broad accent; and the physically handicapped Jonathan Saville who lived in a cottage attached to the chapel in Halifax. Saville preached at South Parade after the minister, Bunting, had refused to bury a Luddite, though he did attend the funeral. Saville was stoned in the street after that, but was never deterred from his earthy offering of the gospel. Of wandering thoughts in prayer he said, 'Nah, ye cannot stop birds flyin' over your 'ead but you can stop 'em buildin' nests in your 'air.' The first year the number of local preachers in Wesleyanism was properly counted was 1883 when there were 17,568. To these many a village chapel owes its existence.

Some local preachers before the bicycle, and the car, might hire a pony and trap or a horse, but many walked miles to appointments, relying, as did the Salisbury preacher featured, on local hospitality, which built up a sense of circuit fellowship. This was still the case when, as a probationer minister in the 1950s, I cycled 3,000 miles a year in rural Essex, which was not unusual.

If one reads the novels of Arnold Bennett such as *The Old Wives' Tale* or *Anna of the Five Towns* one gets a rather grim picture of Wesleyanism in the Potteries. No doubt there was some truth there, but the Wesleyan home and chapel were not devoid of fun. A book by Irene Martin includes a picture of 'chapel' in the early twentieth century (Box 46).

Here is evidence of the very early influence of Westhill College, the Free Church centre of education at Selly Oak, Birmingham where the work of George Hamilton Archibald and later H. A. Hamilton was very influential indeed in all the Free Churches. E. H. Hayes' book *The Child in the Midst* setting up the 'graded' style was published in 1917, so this church was very much 'state of the art' pointing to all sorts of new ways of worship involving children, which were to become very important

---

46. *Chapel 1908*

In September 1908, we very successfully left Yorkshire as father became Superintendent of the Wolverhampton Darlington Street circuit. Our house in Connaught Road was a big one, with a pleasant little garden behind. We went to see 'Wolves' on Saturday afternoons and got to know Kenneth Hunt who played inside right for Wolves and was the son of the Vicar of our parish.

Darlington Street was a large and important church. It had a big evening congregation. Quite a usual thing was to have at least 900 copper coins in the collection plate. There was a choir of 90 people with a very forceful conductor Mr Molyneux, whose son played the organ beautifully. I learned singing from his daughter who was a pupil of Sir Henry Wood. Father was very dissatisfied with the way the Sunday school was run, particularly for the younger children. It was just at the time when the 'grading' of Sunday school was becoming popular – and the idea of having 'Departments' – primary, junior and senior was new. From the Archibalds we learned to run preparation classes.

Source: Irene Martin, *Some of My Memories*, Leeds, 1971.

Miss Martin became a noted biologist. Her brother Sir George Martin was a Leeds businessman and philanthropist.

---

after the Second World War. My father endorsed this description – and added that on St Patrick's Day the boys from Darlington Street Wesleyan Day school and the local Roman Catholic boys would hurl insults at one another – 'Catlickers', 'Wesley bobs' – and even throw bricks!

Other means of grace

There were other 'means of grace' in Wesleyanism besides preaching services and Sunday School worship. The *Watchnight* became common, not now on the night of the full moon but at midnight on New Year's Eve as a counter to pagan activities. This custom was sustained in Halifax into the 1980s. After a New Year's party and the Watchnight we would go on to the street to sing 'Hail Smiling Morn'. *The Covenant Service*[7] was much more sombre and demanding. In the service, which took place normally on the first Sunday of the New Year often in the afternoon, the long exhortation to make an explicit covenant with God (derived from the Puritan Richard Alleine) was followed by a long prayer of dedication originally composed by Joseph Alleine. Lesser poets borrow, great poets steal!

---

47. *The Covenant – part of the affirmation in the 1882 Wesleyan Service Book*

Christ has many services to be done; some are more easy, others more difficult; some bring honour, others bring reproach; some are suitable to our natural inclinations and temporal interests, others are contrary to both. In some we may please Christ, and please ourselves; as when he requires us to feed and clothe ourselves, to provide things honest for our own maintenance, yea, and there are some spiritual duties that are more pleasing than others; as 'to rejoice in the Lord', to bless and praise God, to feed ourselves with the delights and comforts of religion; these are the sweet works of a Christian. But then these are others works wherein we cannot please Christ by denying ourselves; as giving and lending, bearing and forbearing, reproving men for their sins, withdrawing from evil company, witnessing against the wind, swimming against the tide, steering contrary to the times, parting with our ease, our liberties and our accommodations for the name of our Lord Jesus . . . put me to doing, put me to suffering, let me be employed for thee, or laid aside for thee, exalted for thee or trodden under foot for thee; let me be full, let me be empty; let me have all things, let me have nothing; I freely and heartily yield all things to thy pleasure and disposal.

Source: *Order of Administration of the Sacrament and Other Services for the Use of the People called Methodists*, Wesleyan Methodist Book Room, 1883, pp. 54–65.

Wesleyan Methodism used the service with only two revisions, 1879 and 1897, until the *Book of Offices* of 1936.

This service was exceedingly demanding – certainly not for all age worship. The use of the Covenant as a separate service in the afternoon was still the norm at Beckminster Methodist Church, Wolverhampton in the 1950s. It is now normally a morning occasion, usually with participation by the whole congregation and not confined to church members, which raises many questions about its use. It is significant that other churches such as the Church of South India and the Church of Scotland have taken it up. Dr Rowan Williams used some of the more modern version of the Covenant at his installation as Archbishop of Canterbury in 2003.

The Love-feast[8] was still quarterly in some chapels, featuring a very different style of spirituality from either the Covenant Service or Holy Communion. The 'love feast' cup would be handed round, preceded by a style of biscuit specially made. There would be hymns and testimonies, often fervent bursts

---

48. *Love Feast 1910*

Love Feasts were held on the first Sunday of the month in place of the normal evening service. No preacher was in charge. The class leaders were responsible. Hymns and choruses were often struck up by some persons in the pews – popular ones included 'There are angels hovering around', with reference to Mary and Martha . . . Testimonies and prayers were made as those participating felt led. During the meeting two large porcelain, drinking cups inscribed with the words 'Love Feast' were passed from pew to pew each person drinking from them of the water they contained. A shallow basket of buns was also passed round. Collections were made for the poor of the district.

Source: George Sutcliffe, *The History of Mount Tabor Chapel, Halifax 1820–1920*, cited also in K. Young, *Chapel*, London: Eyre Methuen, 1972, pp. 108–9.

Sutcliffe was a local preacher and chemistry teacher.

---

of prayer and charismatic episodes though these became much more infrequent. The Hinde Street Christmas Day (Box 30) can be contrasted with this.

Prayer meetings could be similar, without the water and buns, taking place at different times but often after evening worship when Holy Communion or Love Feast was not celebrated. In many chapels the prayer meetings survived longer than Love Feasts which, except in ecumenical experiments, have largely ceased.

Architecture

We cannot here give a full description of the effects of architecture on worship.[9] If it is true that we shape our buildings but our buildings also shape us, we cannot ignore it. Wesley favoured the octagon style – using the Octagon at Norwich, which was Presbyterian, as a model. Octagon chapels can still be found at Heptonstall (near Hebden Bridge), Yarm and Arbroath. Wesley's Chapel in London was very different with its central pulpit and communion table and rail behind it as in not a few post-Wren Anglican churches. The early nineteenth century saw the building of chapels holding over a thousand people in most large towns. Carver Street, Sheffield (now a pub) had in 1805 as its architect William Jenkins, one of the circuit's itinerant preachers. In 1875 an observer stated that 'Carver Street had an excellent congregation both in quality and quantity, particularly the former . . . last season it had the Mayor and Master Cutler within a few pews of each other. In the main the congregation consists of members of the middle classes, with merchants, manufacturers and professional gentlemen.' In Brunswick, Leeds, the pulpit was astonishingly close to the pews with galleries on three sides and later in 1825 the controversial organ. A preacher of the calibre of Dr Leslie Weatherhead in the 1920s could whisper and be heard by all. The great central pulpits or rostrums with organ behind with the choir seated in front of it became very common.

Methodism had come from the side streets to the centre of towns with municipal buildings to match the Town Halls. There was an element of pride in all this with the names Brunswick, Hanover, or Victoria affirming Methodist loyalty to the state.

The Romantic Movement brought gothic styles back into the Church of England and the expanding Roman Catholic community. A. W. N. Pugin (1812–52) was its chief initiator and inspirer. This style was copied by Dissent, including Methodism with Frederick J. Jobson (1812–81) as its advocate in *Chapel and School Architecture* (1850). Typical of this style was Trinity, Wolverhampton, almost entirely like an Anglican church not only in its use of Morning Prayer but with side pulpit, lectern, choir stalls and communion table under an east end window. Trinity, Bristol, was similar. Yet another mood brought a revival of Byzantine styles with domes – Chorley Old Road, Bolton, was typical of early twentieth century chapels of this style – not to speak of Central Hall, Westminster, which outshone them all. Then came the Central Halls in most towns made to look like 'Halls' not chapels with modern seating and facilities for secular concerts. Later on, just before Methodist union, Crouch, Butler and Savage built several chapels in gothic style in Birmingham, Stourbridge and Wolverhampton – chairs appeared instead of pews.

The great Congregationalist theologian P. T. Forsyth[10] favoured gothic styles for giving a sense of the transcendent, but admitted that it inhibited preaching in the dissenting mode. In all this rivalries between denominations and mill owners were sometimes apparent. How often the large chapels were full is a matter of dispute – 'the myth of the empty chapel' reveals that they were full on special occasions. Far more chapels were built than were really necessary, with the whole problem of debt leading to the need for pew rents and all sorts of money raising efforts, which could be a detriment to evangelism among the poor. We must be honest – it could be expensive to be a Methodist.

For discussion

1. Were the Wesleyans right to have both responsive and extempore prayers?

2. Is the 'preaching service' sometimes called 'the Hymn Sandwich' now a dead duck? If so, why?

3. Should preaching be central in our worship? Why?

4. Do you think Holy Communion is the heart of Christian worship? Is it for you?

5. Is the Covenant Service too demanding?

6. Would you welcome the Love-Feast?

7. Do buildings matter? Why? What style do you prefer?

5

Wesleyanism 1860–1902 Politics, Education and the Forward Movement

Consolidation and change

The devastating events of the 1840s and 1850s were not easy to overcome even if the numbers of Wesleyan members began to grow again. For a time there was a rather conservative mood and the need for money was ever growing in a society which now had half the population in urban areas. Renewed growth, as well as growth in the overseas church, could give Wesleyanism a complacent and triumphalist air, although in relation to population growth there was reason for concern, which the more perceptive leaders realised. They were aware also, of a North to South drift of members, a shift from country to town and from some town centres to the suburbs. Charles Prest (1806–75), a pioneer of Home Missions, noted this as early as 1856.

In some ways the Connexion was to become a kind of solar system with the Conference as the sun with new commissions and committees becoming satellites, like the Chapel Department (1854) and the Home Mission and Contingent Fund (1856). New funds were set up for Scotland (1867), North Wales (1867), South Wales (1873) and for 'Watering Places' – the seaside was becoming a focus for holidays and retirement. What is clear is that these projects were needed to enable Wesleyanism to follow its own members and that powerful laymen were consolidating their influence – Sir Francis Lycett, Sir William McArthur and later the lock and safe manufacturer Sir George H. Chubb and Robert Perks (1849–1934). They instituted a fund for the Extension of Methodism (1874) and the Thanksgiving Fund (1878). Perks, later, initiated the *Twentieth Century Fund* in 1898 to raise one million guineas. It raised, in the end, over £1m – approximately £60m in today's values! Home and Overseas Mission, schools, the Children's Home all benefited but one aim was to build the Central Hall in Westminster as a great headquarters – 'large, central and monumental'. When it opened in 1912, the *Methodist Times* imagined 'an awe-stricken whisper going round the grim gargoyles of the Abbey – the Methodists have come'.

Recent studies have greatly illuminated this period focussing on significant figures, who can represent different issues – Dr James H. Rigg (1821–1909), Principal of Westminster College, London, from 1868 to 1902; Thomas Bowman Stephenson (1839–1912), Hugh Price Hughes (1847–1902) and John Scott Lidgett (1854–1953), whose most notable work will be considered in the next chapter.

J. H. Rigg – Wesleyan style and education

In 1868 the Liberals, led by William Ewart Gladstone, achieved power. By then 'poll books' make clear that most of those Wesleyans who had the vote supported the Liberals. They continued to do so, though there were always some who were Conservatives with an anti-Catholic streak and the group who later formed the Labour Party attracted some Wesleyan support when it moved into national politics – Arthur Henderson (1863–1935) and Jack Lawson (Lord Lawson) (1881–1965) were Wesleyans and local preachers, Henderson becoming Foreign Secretary in 1929. This was only on the horizon in 1868. Increasingly, the Wesleyans on many issues aligned themselves with other Nonconformists. They were not any longer unwilling to be called Nonconformist or later Free Church, a more positive phrase borrowed from Scotland.

The dissenting claims for greater freedom were supported by the Wesleyans. They included the end of compulsory Church Rates (1868) and the admission of dissenters to 'Oxbridge' and Durham universities. It is no coincidence that the liveliest young Wesleyan minister, Hugh Price Hughes, was appointed to Oxford in 1881. Wesley Memorial Church's spire signified a new influence. The sad business of burials in Anglican churchyards saw Methodists such as Perks and his partner H. H. Fowler (1830–1911) supporting the move which gave Free Church ministers the right to conduct burials in churchyards. One angry Rector armed his flock with pitchforks to keep dissenters out. Incidents like that and parliamentary battles did not help the beginnings of an ecumenical spirit. As we have seen, Free Church ministers could, as 'authorised persons', conduct weddings. Wesleyans increasingly celebrated the rites of passage in their own chapels – though some kept up the custom of going to the parish church for these ceremonies.

Internal to Wesleyanism, there was considerable debate about the nature of the Connexion and Conference. Jabez Bunting's view, widely representative, that the ministers in Conference were 'the living Wesley' was becoming impossibly clerical, even to conservatives, though the battle against change was long, led by men like George Osborn (1808–91) who felt the 'satellite' committees gave the laity power enough. Led by Rigg, Stephenson and laymen such as Perks, the matter of proper lay representatives was carried in 1877.[1] From 1878 (when Rigg was President) the Conference was largely selected from the Districts with an equal number of laymen to ministers – 240 of each. There was now a representative session and a pastoral session, which still appointed the President and dealt with matters especially relating to ministers. Increasingly, that session has been restricted, but it was accepted by Primitive Methodists and United Methodists in the negotiations for union. Later, there was a minor sensation when a woman, Miss Dawson, was voted in as a member of the Conference. The 1878 change was highly significant – Conference was no longer 'episcopal' or clerical. It was a representative assembly. Ministers were now seeing their role as far less authoritarian. Methodist union was now a possibility. A Wesleyan Report on the *Nature of the Church* in 1908 clearly pointed in a new direction and was cited by Primitive Methodists when making their case. The mind behind that report was George G. Findlay (1849–1919) of Headingley College, Leeds, representing new styles of biblical scholarship. In 1893 J. H. Rigg proposed that Chairmen of Districts should be set apart as chief pastors and missionaries, a matter not carried out until after the Second World War.

The other great debate was on the nature and discipline of the church. Was the 'class meeting' still determinative of membership and therefore compulsory? J. H. Rigg was 'liberal' on changes in the Conference, but he fought for the class meeting as the heart of Methodism.

The class meeting in which each member spoke of the state of his or her soul each week was becoming stereotyped. For many, it was frankly boring unless the leader was imaginative in questioning and supporting members. Increasingly members were not

49. *The Class – the reality*

The 'class' was a sort of factory processing people for salvation. It was essential that members should be added to it constantly. And that as the class grew, it subdivided and maintained a constant 'put through'. Spiritual decline was inevitable unless people came into the class. By the 1860s . . . the process had slowed down . . . it appears that up to the end of the eighteenth century about 65% of all members met regularly in class. Percentages for the ten years periods . . . are as follows:

1819 – 58%	1869 – 45%
1829 – 56%	1879 – 34%
1839 – 53%	1889 – 23%
1849 – 53%	1899 – 20%
1859 – 46%	

So by the end of the century the disciplinary use of the class had gone with less than a quarter of members meeting in class. The evangelical uses of the class had been taken over by the prayer meeting. (Cf. Newton Flew's view that 50% of London Methodists attended class in 1928.)

Source: William Dean, *Lecture at WHS Conference*, Selly Oak, 1983.

prepared to bare their spiritual bosoms. Also social factors came in – would a middle class lady speak honestly to a harness maker class leader? Increasingly the class meeting, in its origin a system of discipline, its purpose evangelism, had become a 'fellowship' in style.

The debate about the class became crucial. Certainly the class, as David Carter has recently defined it,[2] signified watchfulness, accountability and mutual oversight, which was part of the connexional system, very much seen as necessary not only by Rigg but by the formidable Dr Benjamin Gregory (1820–1900), for years the Connexional Editor and writer of the important *The Holy Catholic Church* of 1873. It is interesting that last century Anglicans such as Bishop E. R. Wickham and Roman Catholics

such as J. M. Todd[3] saw the class meeting as the most distinctive element in Methodism and its loss a catastrophe. In 1894 the *Service for Recognition of New Members* (note the word 'recognition', for 'reception' was by the Leader's meeting in its session) was instituted which was taking Wesleyanism (officially called the Wesleyan Methodist *Church* in 1897) clearly on the road to some form of confirmation, that rite seeking a theology, which the Church of Scotland has also used, so that it is not a Catholic–Anglican monopoly. The nearest approach to the class meeting was to be the Methodist Societies in universities and colleges. They were organised on the class system with leaders responsible for about twelve members – Margaret Thatcher gave her first address in her 'team' at Oxford under Nigel Gilson (President 1986) as leader. House groups have developed and the 'cell' system has increasingly been a feature of other churches, especially the 'New churches', with a disciplinary style which might have appealed to Rigg.

J. H. Rigg in his professional stance as Principal of what became probably the leading teacher training college was involved in many discussions and government initiatives including the Royal Commission on Elementary Education.[4] Gladstone considered him a formidable debater and committee man, Cardinal Manning described him as 'Dr Rigg, Wesleyan but sound' and added 'Dr Dale of Birmingham – unsound'. Rigg felt that Wesleyanism

50. *The Class – in theory*

The Methodist church is a web of class meetings; unloose them and the whole is unravelled. The class meeting is the Matrix note in which every element characteristic of Methodism is nurtured – the class meeting is essential to Methodism. Take it away and there can be no such thing as Methodism.

Source: J. H. Rigg, *The Connexional Economy of Wesleyan Methodism*, Wesleyan Conference Office, 1879, pp. 169, 187.

---

51. *Intolerance in Wales*

The remarkable Evans family of Brynrhedydd Ysceiflog near Holywell, Flintshire provides a striking example of the undue influence of the Established Church in Welsh schools prior to the passing of the 1870 Education Act. During a catechism class in the local school John Hugh, the younger of two brothers who both became leading Wesleyan ministers, was asked by the visiting school inspector: 'What is your name?' When he duly replied 'John Hugh' the subsequent question was 'Who gave you your name?' to which replied 'My father, sir'. The question was repeated by the headmaster who received the same answer. The boy was then commanded to repeat after his teacher: 'My godfather and godmother at my baptism' where upon the eight year old rebel son of a rebellious father again asserted, 'No sir, my father'. For this transgression of law and order, John Hugh was caned. On daringly repeating the offence he was shame-fully beaten in front of the class before the outraged headmaster who summarily dismissed the school. It is little wonder that the boy's father Ioan Tachwedd with the help of other members of local nonconformist chapels forthwith planned, built and opened a 'British' school at nearby Lixwm and that John Hugh with his brother William grew up to be like their father – radical liberals.

Source: L. Madden (ed.), *Methodism in Wales*, Llandudno: Methodist Conference, 2003, p. 110.

---

should retain its 900 day schools if possible – cost was the problem. Education should not be entirely secular, countering the views of R. W. Dale and other Nonconformists who hated the Anglican monopoly of schools in 'single school' areas and the growing number of Roman Catholic schools. State education should be secular, the churches should deal with their own children's religious education, which revealed an optimistic view of the churches' prospects.

At the beginning of the twentieth century, that astute Anglican monk and historian John Neville Figgis said it was strange that the Free Churches wanted entirely secular state schools while the state church wanted free schools. The danger of the Free Church view for Figgis was that there was nothing between individuals and the state. It was the road to 'Leviathan', the totalitarian state. Figgis could point to the entirely secular style in France – in 2004 they seek to keep Muslim headscarves out of schools. Figgis was more prophetic than Dale; Rigg would have agreed with Figgis.

Rigg applauded the Forster Education Act of 1870, which set up the School Boards to administer schools in local areas. Church schools would continue, with support from taxes. The Nonconformists feared that in single school areas, teachers who were not Anglicans would be excluded, a not silly fear. In Wales, especially, fears could be expressed bitterly, especially when in a village the Nonconformist element was overwhelming, a factor leading in the end to Disestablishment under Asquith and Lloyd George. There were 8,000 'single school' areas, and in 1861 the Church of England controlled 19,549 schools. By 1900, the Roman Catholics had 1,000 schools while the Wesleyans in 1902 still had 738 schools with 160,675 pupils.

The 1870 Act had the Cowper-Temple clause insisting on non-denominational religious education in state schools with another clause allowing Nonconformist parents to withdraw their children from offensive religious styles – John Hugh would no longer be beaten, though unpleasant intolerance did not disappear.

Interestingly Rigg co-operated with the leading agnostic T. H. Huxley producing what amounted to

---

52. *Effortless superiority*

When I see my day children are attached to Dissenting Sunday schools I argue that it is a fortunate thing that I can teach them five days our of seven. I know too that the teaching will not be lost. I shall find that, after many days when many of these children leave their sect and seek confirmation.

Source: *The Church Times*, 13 June 1902, p. 5.

an agreed syllabus for London schools with Huxley agreeing that religion should be taught and Rigg agreeing to the teaching of science. Rigg was strongly opposed over the 'Dual System' of state and church schools by the formidable arguments of his friend, William Arthur, representing an Irish viewpoint, but the system has remained.

Methodist education was to greatly expand in this period.[5] Woodhouse Grove School, Bradford, has for long paralleled Kingswood School (now at Bath) but a group of what were called 'middle class' schools appeared, paralleling the Woodard Schools in Anglicanism. The Leys School opened in Cambridge in 1875 with Dr W. F. Moulton (1835–98) as headmaster. Moulton was a fine biblical scholar – some of us still possess a 'Moulton–Geden' Concordance of the New Testament, revised now by Howard Marshall. Moulton was one of the team which produced the Revised Version of the Bible in 1881. The Leys, called the 'Methodist Eton', has an enviable academic prowess, with a concern for the poor also, in the Leysian Mission in London. Wesleyan schools included Queen's College, Taunton (1843); Truro School (1880); Penrhos (1880); Rydal (1885); Culford School (1881); Kent College, Canterbury (1885) with Trinity Hall School, Southport (1872) catering for the daughters of ministers.

All this was a symbol of the growing affluent middle class in Methodism – for the smaller Methodist churches had boarding schools too – wanting educational advantages, which they had not enjoyed. Teacher training grew also with the opening of Southlands College for the training of women teachers. David Martin, the sociologist, was not exaggerating when he claimed that 'the central figure for teaching Christianity is a lady in a primary school. By a happy chance for Christianity those who teach in primary schools are amongst the most well disposed to the faith and most strongly practising of all social strata.'[6] Smaller private schools were presided over by women of the calibre of Miss Rigg (daughter of J. H. Rigg) at the Mary Datchelor School and Miss Hannah Pipe at Laleham. Katherine Barratt – later wife of Hugh Price Hughes

– was deeply influenced by Miss Pipe's willingness sometimes to be a reverent agnostic.

We must add new theological colleges at Headingley, Leeds and Handsworth, Birmingham, where for a time Robert Young combined his tutorship with being Secretary of the Conference. Later, links with the new universities were to be established by all the colleges.

Mission alongside the poor – T. B. Stephenson

Thomas Bowman Stephenson was a pioneer in Wesleyan concern for the poor. It if often said that the famous pamphlet of 1883 *The Bitter Cry of Outcast London* sparked the churches into action. That was so, but Stephenson was active long before that. When minister at Fletcher Street, Bolton, in 1865, he noted the plight of the poor, especially children. He also employed a Miss Entwistle as 'Deaconess', a rare use then of the word. Moving to London he noted the reality of poverty.

Aided by Alfred Mager and Francis Horner, Stephenson founded the *Children's Home* in Church Street, Lambeth, becoming its Principal in 1873. His organisation was greatly influenced by the work of Theodor Fliedner at Kaiserswerth. Although he was

---

53. *London poverty*

I soon saw the little children in a condition, which made my heart bleed. There they were shoeless, filthy, their faces pinched with hunger and premature wretchedness staring out of their too bright eyes, and I began to feel that now my time had come. Here were my poor little brothers and sisters sold to hunger and the devil and I could not be free of their blood if I did not at least try to save some of them.

Source: W. Bradfield, *Life of T. B. Stephenson*, Kelly, 1913, p. 78. Also E. Dorothy Graham, *Saved to Serve: The Story of the Wesley Deaconess Order 1890–1978*, Werrington: Methodist Publishing House, 2002, p. 415.

no mere imitator, the word 'Home' was carefully chosen. Its object was to create a family atmosphere. Prominent Wesleyans such as John Chubb, Francis Lycett and Sir William McArthur supported his work, which was comparable with that of Thomas Barnardo. Branches of the Children's Home were opened at Bonner Road (1871) and at Edgworth, near Bolton, in 1872. Crowthorn School, there, was maintained as a centre for handicapped children until 2002. The home at Birmingham – Princess Alice Orphanage – followed in 1882. Stephenson pioneered the training of those working with children by the order of *Sisters of the Children* who held their first workers' conference in 1878. A logical development of his work with children was the founding of the *Wesley Deaconess Institute*.[7] Its concept was an order 'with vocation but no vow, discipline without servility, association not excluding freedom'. Mewburn House in east London was the first headquarters of the Institute set up in 1890 predating the official foundation of the Order by twelve years. There were soon branches at Norwich and Leicester. In 1900 Stephenson resigned from the Principalship of the Children's Home, which now had considerable – and somewhat controversial – work in Canada and became known as *The National Children's Home and Orphanage* (NCHO now NCH). He became Superintendent minister at Ilkley and Warden of the Deaconess Institute set up there. It is a tribute to Stephenson's vision and acumen that both of these institutions he founded still flourish in new styles. In the year of his death 2,201 children were cared for by the NCHO and there were 229 Wesley Deaconesses who were to be joined at Methodist union by similar groups in the other Methodist churches. The sheer variety in a world setting of the Wesley Deaconess order is a great story. The parallel *Sisters of the People*, set up in Manchester in 1890 by S. F. Collier and in London by Katherine Price Hughes, brought some exceedingly able women seeking new vocations into the work of Wesleyanism.

Before we leave Stephenson, we must note that he pioneered ecumenism in the Methodist Church

---

54. *Deaconesses in 1901*

Of the 71 Deaconesses and Probationers now in active service two are in charge of Training Houses, two are Deaconess-Evangelists, and two have devoted themselves to the establishment and management of a Convalescent Home for poor women and children. Three are Deaconess-Nurses of whom one is connected with Calvert House, one is on the staff of a circuit and one is labouring with a Great Mission. Five Deaconesses hold appointments beyond the seas; one of whom is establishing an affiliated order in New Zealand; two are in the Transvaal and two are toiling amid the darkness of a thoroughly heathen village in Ceylon. Fourteen deaconesses are working in connection with Home Mission in England, Scotland and Ireland and forty-three are connected with circuits. Nearly all of these last are engaged in work of a missionary character. They are seeking to revive decayed causes or to nurse young ones. In a few cases they are strengthening the pastoral work need amongst large congregations.

Source: E. Dorothy Graham, *Saved to Save*, p. 2; cf. J. Banks, *The Story So Far: The First 100 Years of the Manchester and Salford Methodist Mission*, 1986, ch. 6.

---

as an absolute necessity at the World Methodist Conference of 1901.

Stephenson's work among deaconesses was followed by William Bradfield from 1907 to 1920 and Russell Maltby from 1920 to 1940. J. A. Findlay in 1928 heard someone ask the Archbishop of York, William Temple: 'Your Grace, what religious leader has most effectively appealed to the student classes in recent years?' Immediately Temple replied 'Without any exception of any sort, unquestionably Maltby'.

The Forward Movement – Hugh Price Hughes[8]

Methodism had an itinerant system of ministry from Wesley's time. Ministers in the late nineteenth century still moved every three years. J. H. Rigg compared a connexional system with independency when the minister could be at the beck and call of wealthy lay people. He had a point, although it was not fair to the contemporary strength of urban Congregationalism. He was stressing the mutual accountability of ministry to a wider church than the local church. There was here a real equality of stipend and what the French call *disponibilité* – a willingness, at least ideally, to be stationed anywhere from Land's End to the Shetlands, not to speak of the Mission Field. What of inner cities, what of the need for new styles of ministry, of which District Missionaries were a symptom of new change? Here we feature Hugh Price Hughes, though he was not always the pioneer even if his newspaper *The Methodist Times* sometimes gave that impression.

Hughes combined the holiness tradition with a radical, though not socialist, style owing much to the theology of the Anglican F. D. Maurice, even if he criticised his style, and to the philosophy of T. H. Green, the brooding Oxford figure behind new forms of liberal political thought. If the state had the task of removing obstacles to freedom, these to Hughes included the evils of 'slavery, drunkenness, the social evil [impurity and prostitution], ignorance, pauperism, mammon and war'. That list of evils remained the touchstone of much of his work.

Hughes took up the polemic of the Quaker John Bright that 'what is morally wrong can never be politically right', leading to his demand (along with others, including Roman Catholics) that men such as Charles Dilke, a rising Liberal, and the Irish leader Charles Stewart Parnell were not fit to be politicians, because they were guilty of adultery. He and Dr Henry Lunn (1859–1939), who treated him as a mentor, protested at the style of the Wesleyan Methodist Missionary Society, especially in relation to education policy in India, claiming that it was not producing Christians and that the missionaries were enjoying a lifestyle which set them apart from Indian people. J. H. Rigg, W. L. Watkinson and

C. H. Kelly felt that Lunn was acting unworthily. It was a complex and unpleasant controversy raising issues far beyond Wesleyanism.

Hughes was a pioneer of the *National Council of the Evangelical Free Churches*, of which he was the first President in 1896. He believed the church of the future would be Methodism across the British Empire and the USA. The 'New Imperialism' of this time was supported by prominent Methodists such as Perks and Hughes who saw the British Empire as a great liberating force to 'backward peoples', supporting the Boer War (1899–1902) as a way of freeing the Bantu from the followers of Kruger, and earlier supporting a crusade against the Turks.

Much earlier, Hughes had joined in the battle against the Contagious Diseases Act along with Josephine Butler. The Act had allowed women to be medically examined, forcibly if necessary, if accused of prostitution. We could examine many more controversies of the period when Hughes led the West London Mission from 1887 until his death in 1902. The day before the massive stroke which killed him, he rather sadly wrote of his early

---

55. *The Boer War*

We hope it is not mere racial prejudice which compels us to believe that the Englishman, with all his faults, treats the natives of Africa more kindly and justly than the Dutchman. After all, that is a great moral issue. Englishmen and Dutchmen together are a significant minority in the midst of vast multitudes of Africans. Which is most likely to promote the civilisation and evangelisation of the natives of the soil? Is there not a Providence in the history of our relation to Africa, notwithstanding all our sins? Is it not our duty in the last resort, however reluctantly and sadly, to insist upon the ascendancy of the English race in South Africa, in the general interests of mankind?

Source: *The Methodist Times*, 24 August 1899. C. Oldstone-Moore, *Hugh Price Hughes*, Cardiff: University of Wales Press, 1999, p. 312. Cf. p. 323.

---

56. *Has Methodism a future?*

Whether Methodism is to dwindle away into a narrow stereotyped feeble sect, or grow into a great church, a worthy mother of the great Methodist communities beyond the seas. If the conference should deliberately resolve that Methodism can do nothing for the vast multitudes of London, outside the ordinary circuit system with its absorbing detail and its ceaseless change of pastorate, we shall witness the beginning of the end. The young, the gifted, the ardent will drift away to churches that have sufficient life and sufficient faith in God to subordinate all methods and all interests to the supreme end of evangelizing the nation.

Source: *The Methodist Times*, 18 March 1886, pp. 1–2; Oldstone-Moore, p. 156.

---

enthusiasms – 'But today, well people read the *Daily Mail*'. His most recent biographer summed him up as a 'compound of insight and error, achievement and failure'. Let us look at two areas where he was prominent.

The Forward Movement can be said to represent the last great attempt to reach those alienated from all the churches. Historians have recently insisted that there was much vaguely evangelical 'folk religion' through the influence of Sunday Schools and other agencies into which evangelists could tap. The leaders of the movement included H. J. Pope (1836–1912), Charles Garrett (1823–1900) who pioneered the Manchester Lay Mission and later the Liverpool Mission in 1875 with four lay missionaries, and Samuel Collier (1859–1921) whose work at Manchester after 1886 was parallel to that of Hughes in London.[9] These men shared Hughes' vision that they must not only seek to save people's souls but 'sanctify their circumstances'; the sacrament and the soup ladle would go hand in hand.

Charles Booth in his *Life and Labour in London* (1903), following William Booth's *In Darkest England and the Way Out* – recalling darkest Africa – and the researches of Rowntree in York showed that 30% of the population were living below an adequate subsistence level. Drunkenness was a fearful social evil when six shillings could buy 31 pints of beer in 1901. A minister needed to be long enough in an area to be a social and, for some, a political as well as an evangelistic force. This was the basis of centres like St James Hall (later Kingsway Hall), the Manchester and Salford Mission and the Central Halls in Bolton (2,400 in the evening congregation in 1906), Birmingham led by Luke Wiseman, Edinburgh, Glasgow and Leeds presided over by Samuel Chadwick as well as the significant centres in the East End of London with Peter Thompson outstanding. The last of the first group of central Missions were at Newcastle, Sunderland, and Nottingham in 1902 but many more were to follow until the Second World War.

Collier's work at Manchester can be taken as an example. The Mission claimed to have the largest Methodist congregation in the world with at least 16,000 people at all services and in 1902 some 3,521 members, though some decline due to population change was to follow. Collier soon found that evangelism was not enough. He had 2,500 voluntary workers operating a Men's Home and a Labour Yard to give employment, a Women's and Maternity Home, a shelter for cripples, and choirs and orchestras as well as schools and Bands of Hope. His Sisters of the People remained a feature of the Mission until 1936 when they amalgamated with the Wesley Deaconess order. The Central Halls were first of all evangelistic centres. The preacher was still at the centre and the preacher expected conversions as Hughes did in the evenings after his political and prophetic ovations in the afternoons. J. E. Rattenbury, one of his distinguished successors, combined much of the same styles (see Box 57).

Rattenbury's last point about the decline of belief in Hell contrasts with the recent assertion of Michael Watts that it stultified evangelism. A missioner like Samuel Chadwick at Leeds always backed up evangelism with groups of various kinds – including one for those who wished to learn New Testament Greek and one for those who wanted to improve

<hr>

57. *Rattenbury on evangelism in 1910 and 1960*

In any congregation, normal or otherwise, sixty five years ago you could count on a general sense of guilt, now the only thing you can count on is a general sense of doubt. Guilt is like tinder which blazes when the spark of emotion is applied to it, doubt is like a rust which can only be removed by careful polishing.

Rattenbury reflected on the *Welsh Revival of 1904–5*: 'It spread like a fire through Wales but it was unfortunately over-publicized by the new journalism. I think it might be called the last of the revivals of the old evangelism and was not affected to any extent by the loss of belief in Hell. The permanent effect of it was, I think, neutralized by the out-of-date Puritanism of the Welsh sects.'

Source: Donald Soper, *The Advocacy of the Gospel*, London: Hodder and Stoughton, 1961, p. 18; J. E. Rattenbury, *Evangelism and Pagan England*, London: Epworth Press, 1954, pp. 25, 31ff on Hughes.

<hr>

their cricket – this was, after all, Yorkshire! He showed, too, a concern for housing policy in the city. Growth in discipleship in the Missions was followed up by social witness of a basically individualistic kind, despite avowals of collectivism. The danger was that social witness was spilling over into a desire, perhaps unconscious at times, to manipulate and dominate the Liberal Party and impose their brand of morality on the wider society. David Bebbington succinctly summarised what *The Times* in 1890, commenting on the Parnell affair, called 'The Nonconformist Conscience': 'There is no strict boundary between religion and politics, an insistence that politicians should be men of the highest character and a belief that the state should promote the moral welfare of its citizens.' The pitfall was trying to impose a moral discipline that would not endure unless it was voluntarily agreed upon by society at large. Prohibition of alcohol was one example. The Parnell case is another illustration. It spoiled Hughes' support for Irish Home Rule,

which had already split the Liberal Party and divided Nonconformity, which divided again on the Boer War, although the Free Church Federal Council did seek a peace process, which is often forgotten.

Another feature of the Forward Movement was what Dr Tudur Jones called 'the fellowship of activity', the creation of cultural or semi-cultural groups and interests around the church or hall which, now, can be seen either as a broadening of

<hr>

58. *The Wesley Guild*

The Guild's later motto was 'One heart, one way' with the four C's – comradeship, consecration, culture and Christian service. Weekly meetings would normally be a) a monthly devotional meeting; b) literary meeting; c) social and musical evening; d) Bible reading, literary meeting or lecture.

Number of Guilds:
1897 – 620, membership 34,017
1900 – 1,130, membership 75,154
1906 – 1,920, membership 132,228
1928 – 3,829, membership 208,607

Very notable was the Ilesha Hospital in Nigeria, sponsored by the Guild, and the notable work of the Holiday Homes and the recent Nigeria Health Care Project. *A testimony*. 'It was in the Tonypandy Methodist Central Hall that I belonged to the Wesley Guild in the 1920s and 1930s. My first effort at public speaking was to give a paper on my favourite book – *The Mill on the Floss* to the Wesley Guild. My hands shook as I stood in front of my friends to read my paper. How I loved the Guild. The friends I made there were to be my lifelong friends. The Wesley Guild contribution within Methodism cannot be measured.' It should be added that the *International Bible Reading Association* much supported by Methodists, was an offshoot of the Wesley Guild.

Source: W. Leary, *The Wesley Guild: The First Hundred Years*, 1996, p. 1.

Reflections of George Thomas, Lord Tonypandy – Speaker of the House of Commons.

the church's outreach or a creeping secularisation of church life, since, in the end, secular groups would be able to provide greater facilities and more money. But *Pleasant Sunday Afternoons* (PSA) was popular – 'bright, brief and brotherly', leading to the Brotherhood Movement, strong in the north east. The parallel meetings for women and the Bands of Hope were typical of the period, very different from class meetings or Love Feasts. The *Wesley Guild* was pioneered by W. B. FitzGerald (1856–1931) supported by C. H. Kelly. It proved to be a very successful method of reaching a generation of young people.[10]

This represents a style of evangelism, which I would call evangelism by friendship, which became characteristic of much modern Methodism such as the Youth Club movement of the Second World War. Cliff College maintained a more traditional revivalist style including the friar-like 'Trekkers' of the 1920s. Meanwhile the political style of Hugh Price Hughes died with the strange death of the Liberal Party at the end of the First World War.

For discussion

1. Should we have retained our 'faith schools'?

2. Should the churches maintain fee-paying public schools?

3. What is the role of Central Missions now?

4. Have the churches lost their influence in the university at student and academic level? Why do the Evangelicals seem now more successful?

5. Was it right to replace the Wesley Deaconess Order by the Diaconal Order? What *is* the role of the Deacon?

6. How does the church seek to help community development and the poor in your area? Alcoholics? Drug addicts? Ethnic minorities? Asylum seekers?

Chronology 1860–1902

Wesleyanism	The Wider World
1861 The *Methodist Recorder*	1861 American Civil War
	1861 Death of Prince Albert
	1862 Cotton Famine
	1864 Papal Syllabus of Errors
	1867 Second Reform Act
	1867 First Lambeth Conference
1868 Headingley College, Leeds	1868–74 Gladstone's Liberal Government
1869 National Children's Home	1869 Disestablishment of Church of Ireland
	1870 First Vatican Council
	1870 Forster Education Act
	1870 Franco-Prussian War
	1871 University Tests abolished
1872 Southlands College	1872 Licensing Act
1872 Trinity Hall School for Girls	
1875 The Leys School	1875 Moody and Sankey Mission
1877 New Hymn Book	1877 Parnell, President of Home Rule Confederation
1878 Laymen admitted to Conference	
	1880 Burial Law Amendment Act
1881 Handsworth College, Birmingham	1881 First Methodist Ecumenical Conference
1882 New Service Book	
	1883 'Bitter Cry of Outcast London'
1883 Manchester Mission	
1885 *Methodist Times*	
1886 West London Mission	
	1888 Third Lambeth Conference
	1890 Parnell resigns as Leader of Irish Party
	1893 Irish Home Rule defeated in Lords
1894 Service for New Members	
1894 Wesley Deaconess Institute	
1896 Wesley Guild	
1898 Twentieth Century Fund launched	
	1899–1902 The Boer War
1902 Death of Hugh Price Hughes	

6

Wesleyanism 1902–32

The beginning of a new century – a survey

Was Britain still the centre of the world? Would its Empire endure? Would Methodism be the church of the new century as Hugh Price Hughes, who died in 1902, hoped as he looked at the USA and the parts of the globe marked in red? Was Rudyard Kipling, who Hughes claimed was not wholly free of his Wesleyan upbringing, more realistic in his Recessional of 1897? He celebrated Empire but gave a dire warning.

---

59. *Empire 1897*

> Far-called, our navies melt away,
> On dune and headland sinks the fire;
> Lo! All our pomp of yesterday
> Is one with Nineveh and Tyre!
> Judge of the Nations, spare us yet
> Lest we forget; let we forget!

Source: *Methodist Hymn Book* 1933, No. 889, cf. No. 899.

That two Kipling poems should be there is interesting.

Empire Day might be celebrated on 24 May – Queen Victoria's birthday – but Germany and the USA were already becoming stronger economically. There were ominous signs of economic and social problems, not least in Ireland. The mood of the Free Churches was buoyant. Who could foresee that by 1990, a historian would write: 'The decline of English nonconformity as a major part of English culture in the twentieth century may well be seen as profound a change in English history as the suppression of the monasteries under Henry VIII'? Yet he also claims: 'Nonconformity . . . has so far permeated English life in the twentieth century that the nonconformist legacy has affected millions who have never set foot in a chapel'.[1] I have chosen the year 1902 as this was the year of the controversial Education Act which set secondary education on a proper basis. It so enraged some Free Church people since it appeared to support Anglican and Roman Catholic schools by allocating money from the local rates (now the Council Tax) continuing the dual system. Again, who could foresee that the system would still operate over a century later? As the Wesleyans still maintained 750 day schools, Conference adopted a more moderate tone than other Free Churches including the Primitive Methodists (see Box 60).

Charles H. Kelly (1833–1911), who had successfully put Wesleyanism much more on the publishing map in what became the *Epworth Press*, and Luke Wiseman (1858–1944) at the Birmingham Mission, were not complacent about Methodist prospects. They noted that membership was not keeping up with population growth. Kelly, who had supported the Wesley Guild, wondered if Methodism was appealing to a younger generation, noting the ageing of congregations in relation to their neighbourhoods.

The characteristic leader of Wesleyanism in the early years of the century – still active during the Second World War – was John Scott Lidgett[2] who

60. *The Wesleyan Conference on the Education Bill of 1902*

The Conference once more declares that the primary object of Methodist policy in the matter of Elementary Education is the establishment of School Boards everywhere acting in districts of sufficient area and the placing of a Christian unsectarian school within reasonable distance of every family. The Conference, therefore, deeply regrets that the present Education Bill is intended to destroy the School Board System and to make no adequate provision for the just claims of those parents who do not desire their children to be driven into denominational schools. The Conference has no wish to abolish the denominational schools or to prevent them being used, with equitable restrictions for the purpose of giving denominational education to those children whose parents desire it. But the Conference expresses once more its deep conviction that no increased grant is accompanied by adequate and representative public management. If, however, denominational schools are to be almost wholly maintained from imperial taxes and local rates, the irreducible minimum of the rights of conscience and of public justice demands that at least a majority of the Local Education Authority (LEA) and of the governing committee of every school shall consists of publicly elected persons.

Source: *Minutes of Wesleyan Methodist Conference*, 1902.

pioneered and lived at the Bermondsey Settlement from 1892 to 1949.

Scott Lidgett represented the reasonably radical Liberalism, which had David Lloyd George as its national leader. Lidgett practised what he preached on the London County Council and in London University, being Vice-Chancellor the year before Methodist union in 1932 and becoming the first President of the new church, having been President of the Wesleyan Methodist Church in 1908, when he was deeply involved in educational controversy, along with the Head of the Education Committee in Asquith's Government, Sir Walter Runciman (1847–1937), who was a Wesleyan. They failed to secure great changes in the Education Act. Lidgett, too, attacked the House of Lords trenchantly for prevaricating over drink legislation. He had the prescience to realise the significance of the rise of the Labour Party in 1906, even if it was the year of the Liberal Party's great triumph at the polls. It seemed that Dissent would, at last, be able to achieve maximum power and influence. Lidgett, in the end, had to see the Liberal–Nonconformist alliance virtually disappear, when the First World War saw Wesleyanism become very much part of the 'Establishment' on issues of peace and war. There was a small pacifist minority led by Samuel Keeble (1853–1946), whose own short-lived *Methodist Weekly* had marked his break from Hugh Price Hughes, years before.

Methodism was inevitably changing its style. Many had seen the chapel as the centre of their life, where they spent much time finding their friends and marriage partners. Now there were wider horizons and contacts through social mobility and education. Christian values were not always normative. At Manchester University, James Hope Moulton (1863–1917) became, as we have seen, an authority on other faiths, no longer concluding that they were to be overthrown by the evangelization of the world in one generation as the noted American Methodist J. R. Mott triumphantly (to us now!) put it. New styles of ministerial training were needed, a matter pioneered by Moulton's fellow Professor at Manchester, the Primitive Methodist layman Arthur S. Peake (1865–1929). No longer was Darwinism a concept ignored – W. H. Dallinger (1842–1909) had openly supported it in his controversial Fernley Lecture of 1887 – *The Creator and What We May Know of the Method of Creation*, despite criticism which was turned on tutors such as Agar Beet (1840–1924) and later George Jackson (1864–1924), who had earlier pioneered work at the Edinburgh Mission in 1888 and became a member of the staff at Didsbury College, Manchester despite an attempt to arraign him on a charge of heresy.[3]

Perceptive and wealthy lay people such as Michael Guttridge and William Greenhalgh were later to assist John H. Ritson (1868–1953) in funding chairs in the existing colleges, to equip chapels there, and later, in 1921, to found Wesley House in Cambridge with Maldwyn Hughes (1875–1940) as its first Principal. The colleges were no longer afraid of modern methods of biblical scholarship and were soon to share in a renaissance of Free Church scholarship, which continued for a generation. It was at Cambridge that the 'Methodist Society' led by Harold Beales (1886–1967), with Harold Roberts (1896–1982) pioneering similar work at Oxford, began to reveal the growing number of students with Methodist backgrounds entering universities as was the case, too, with the Roman Catholics. Young men such as Herbert Butterfield (1900–79) and Charles Coulson (1910–74) became Fellows of their colleges and local preachers before Methodist union, a portent of considerable influence after the Second World War in history and science, a lay contribution with a distinctly Methodist flavour about it. This was beginning to mean a different constituency in the chapels too. The First World War alienated some of the younger generation who would no longer tolerate an obsession with teetotalism and domination by an older style.

Methodism was still declining in relation to population, though there was a slight increase of Wesleyan numbers in the mid 1920s attributed to a later spurt of aggressive evangelism by Rodney (Gipsy) Smith (1860–1947) and others. Some Central Halls still had wide ministries of evangelism and social concern.

Wesleyanism still had its greatest strength in the West Riding of Yorkshire and 12.9% of its members there with 12% of the membership in Lancashire. Middlesex and London had 7.7%, showing growth through migration, although Methodism was acquiring a southern strength as the century wore on. As late as 1961, apart from Cornwall and the Isle of Wight, the main numerical strength of Methodism lay in the northern half of England with a growing suburban style. The 'labour aristocracy' was making way for the new professions – clerks, teachers and nurses jostling with the shopkeepers and engineers. In a town such as Horwich in Lancashire this change is very noticeable. The other Methodist Connexions

---

61. *The aims of the Bermondsey Settlement*

The main objective of the Settlement was to bring a force of educated workers to give help to all the higher interests of the neighbourhood, religious, educational, social and administrative. Its aims were defined at the outset in the following terms:

1. To bring additional force and attractiveness to the Christian work.
2. To become a centre of social life, where all classes may meet together on equal terms for healthful intercourse and recreation.
3. To give facilities for the study of Literature, History, Science and Art.
4. To bring men together to discuss general and special social evils and to seek their remedy.
5. To take such part in local administration and philanthropy as may be possible.
6. And so to do all this that it shall be perfectly clear that no mere sectarian advantage is sought, but that it shall be possible for all good men to associate themselves with our work.

It is clear from all that has been said that the Settlement differs considerably in aim and therefore in development from a Mission. A Settlement is or should be a community of social workers who come to a poor neighbourhood to assist by the methods of friendship and co-operation those who are concerned in upholding all that is essential to the well being of the neighbourhood. Hence freedom and initiative are of its essence. Men and women who come to it must be encouraged to see with their own eyes and to respond with a large measure of independence to the calls that are made upon them. A cut-and-dried programme would be fatal both to the conception and to the development of a settlement. Its head should not stereotype but guide and co-ordinate all its activities, encouraging adventure, though tempering it with prudence.

Source: J. Scott Lidgett, *Reminiscences*, London: Epworth Press, 1928, pp. 21–31. For full details of the Bermondsey settlement see Alan Turberfield, *John Scott Lidgett*, Werrington: Epworth Press, 2003.

were becoming similar in social structure so that the movement for union, which took up so much energy after the war made it imperative to bring together the denominations, which shared still a legacy of theology and style from Wesley's evangelical Arminianism, which still marked them off a little from the other Free Churches, which pursued rather innocuous ideas of Federation. Argument about the representative nature of ordained ministry had become possible after the change in Conference in 1878. This made a wider union viable, especially after the union in 1907 of the UMFC, the MNC and the Bible Christians. What had been flagged up as a

---

62. *A typical mission at the time of Methodist Union – Oxford Place, Leeds*

In 1935, just after Methodist Union, there were 7 centres. Oxford Place Chapel near the Town Hall; Isle Lane Chapel; Holbeck; Central Hall – New Wortley; Mint Chapel; Hanover Square Chapel, Pottery Field, Bethel.

  4,000 men and women attend Sunday services.
  2,500 Sunday School scholars.
   600 Working girls lunch in Home Room (Oxford Place) weekly.
   500 workless and homeless men received bed and shelter tickets in 1934.
   400 members in Women's Meetings.
   180 unemployed men entertained in New Year.
   300 girls and boys attend children's cinema.
  1,236 church members (in Full Membership).
   112 'On Trial' for membership.
    2 unemployed recreational centres.
Fellowship and Prayer Meetings. Factory services. Prison work. Open air work. Hospitals visited. Men's Institutes and girls' clubs. Holiday outings. Staff and voluntary visitation. Boy Scouts and Girl Guide organizations. Work Daily etc etc.

Source: *The Centenary of Oxford Place Chapel, Leeds 1835–1935.*

Note: The work of Samuel Chadwick was continued by notable missioners.

---

63. *Arthur Henderson 1908, 1929*

No longer were they satisfied with seeking to lead an individual to patient resignation . . . the doctrine of contentment had given way to one divine discontent. When he said that 'the workers had more to fear from the evils of drink and gambling than from capitalism' some union members were furious. He replied 'that he wanted to liberate them from both the capitalist and the brewer'. In 1929 he said that the Labour Movement 'received much of its driving force and inspiration from radical Nonconformity' and that the bulk of Labour MPs 'had graduated into their wider sphere of activity via the Sunday school, the bible class, the temperance society or the pulpit'.

Source: C. Wrigley, *Arthur Henderson*, University of Wales Press, 1990; Mary A. Hamilton, *Arthur Henderson*, London: Heinemann, 1938; Alan Wilkinson, *Christian Socialism: Scott Holland to Tony Blair*, London: SCM Press, 1998, pp. 210ff.

---

necessity by T. B. Stephenson in 1901 was now an achievable goal.

Methodism in all its forms was supportive of the Free Church Councils set up in 1896 and 1919 and was able, as we shall see, to play a lively part in response to the Lambeth Conference *Appeal to All Christian People* of 1920, even if Lidgett was disappointed at its consequences. Later Methodism, very early on, espoused the scheme for the Church of South India, revealing that an episcopal system was possible for non-Anglican churches.

Politically, Wesleyanism was supportive of the Liberal party as it had been for a generation – longer in Wales. There were a growing number like Sir George Chubb who found allegiance to conservatism more congenial than what seemed the old-fashioned style of men like Sir Isaac Foot (1880–1960). Some were National Liberals like Alderman Roberts, Margaret Thatcher's father. A very articulate number moved from radical Liberalism to the Labour Party with the significant Primitive Methodist trade union constituency playing an interesting role in the General Strike of 1926, alienating some of the more radical union leaders who were moving in a Marxist direction. Arthur Henderson was representative of Christian socialism, which lay behind the claim by Morgan Phillips, Secretary of the Labour Party, in 1951 that 'the Labour Party was more Methodist than Marxist', a sentiment repeated recently by Prime Minister Tony Blair, no doubt for reasons of his own.

In social policy a mildly collectivist view of the state was replacing older pietism. The 'no politics' rule had changed out of all recognition, although Wesleyanism for some still had the feel of a group with a predictable stress on personal morality and moral crusading with total abstinence – and indeed prohibition. This was still advocated in almost automatic Conference resolutions in the 1920s, sponsored by John Alfred Sharp (1856–1932) who was President of Conference in 1921.

Fundamental social change was the aim of the

---

64. *Methodism: the view of Nathan Söderblom, Archbishop of Sweden, 1919*

1. Methodism which has become the most characteristic form of religion in the New World – Luther's evangelical certainty of faith translated into soul sufficing intensity and Anglo-Saxon capability of action. (Was this true of Britain also?)

Source: W. A. Visser't Hooft, *The Genesis and Formation of the World Council of Churches*, Geneva: WCC, 1981.

2. These reorderings of society were, at root, changes in lifestyle and values, as well as economic changes. They reconstituted local hierarchies and made it possible for the middling sort of people to persuade the poor and dependent to adopt their style of life. The local elites which emerged often wanted to institute a purer, more regular lifestyle. This promoted a kind of 'Global Methodism' in the broadest sense of the term.

Source: C. A. Bayly, *The Birth of the Modern World, 1780–1914*, Oxford: Blackwell, 2004, p. 474.

Wesleyan Methodist Union of Social Service with its magazine *See and Serve* published from 1906 to 1917. It was very much influenced by the formidable W. F. Lofthouse (1871–1965) of Handsworth College and Henry Carter (1874–1951) who came into his own after Methodist union. Samuel Keeble was very active with books such as *Industrial Day Dreams* (1896) and his Fernley Lecture of 1922 *Christian Responsibility for the Social Order*. He led the *Sigma Club* of 1909, avowedly socialist, which included some powerful future leaders including J. E. Rattenbury, A. W. Harrison (later Principal of Westminster College), Maldwyn Hughes, Lofthouse and Moulton. Keeble's Fernley lecture was a Methodist 'trailer' to the *Conference on Christian Politics, Economics and Citizenship* (COPEC) at Birmingham in 1924 in which Wesleyans played a significant role. Some have seen it as a blueprint for the Welfare State (a phrase used by William Temple at that time) to be established after the Second World War. Bleak years of depression were to come, not to speak of the rise of Hitler.

Politics and the effect of war

It has been argued that the First World War marked the end of the Victorian age, and that the war marked the end of Free Church influence on national politics. The Free Churches had become, effectively, part of the Establishment with the King present at a Free Church Thanksgiving Service after the end of the conflict. The war itself caused no surprise to prophetic figures such as J. N. Figgis but was a surprise, apparently, to Winston Churchill. We must confine ourselves to Wesleyanism, which in the war had its own chaplaincy service, going back to the battles of Dr W. H. Rule (1802–90) to secure Wesleyan chaplains against considerable Anglican opposition. There was a strong element in Wesleyanism in favour of the war, considered a 'just war' after the German invasion of Belgium. While more Primitive Methodists took a pacifist line, very quickly they too, saw the war as a battle

65. A chaplain speaks

We could hold no services but none the less, the chaplains were busy about their Master's business. To them no service was too menial, no task ever came amiss. They washed the swollen, filthy feet of the foot-sore infantry, the white-haired Bickerstaff-Drew (the Roman Catholic chaplain), on bended knees, swabbed up the blood-stained floor of a dressing station; they helped the doctors with the wounded, lent a hand to carry a stretcher, rode ahead to choose bivouac or billets and then guided the unit to its place of rest. These were the things, which brought us close to our men and opened their hearts to us so that we could minister to their spiritual needs. But most precious and most sacred was the service rendered to the dying and when the end came, the last sad office of the dead.

Source: Owen Spencer Watkins (1873–1957), Senior Wesleyan Chaplain to the Forces and later Deputy Chaplain General; John Smyth, *In this Sign Conquer: the Story of Army Chaplains*, Oxford: Mowbray, 1968, p.161; Alan Wilkinson, *Dissent or Conform: War, Peace and the English Churches*, London: SCM Press, 1986, p. 79.

for civilisation and righteousness, leading to something like a guilt complex when the appalling conflict and loss of life led to forms of appeasement later.[4]

In 1917 Arthur Henderson left the War Cabinet because he supported socialist conferences which could include neutral and German delegates.

While chaplains such as Owen Spencer Watkins and the Primitive Methodist R. F. Wearmouth, whose *Pages From a Padre's Diary* is a fine account, were in the trenches, the Conference had to make its statement on the war in 1915 (see Box 67).

Conscientious objection took on new significance after the introduction of conscription in 1916. The number of deaths of British men was horrendous – 740,000 – nine per cent of all men under forty, including 16,000 Wesleyans. This clearly affected the churches (look at war memorials) though church membership did not at this point show any rapid decline. The report *The Army and Religion* made

church leaders realise the impact on a whole generation, who not surprisingly became disillusioned with the Christian faith and the church. As far as local churches were concerned the impact on the number of young men was great – greater in Great Britain than in the Second World War, except in areas where the 'Blitz' demolished and destroyed many buildings, killing civilians in a way different from

66. Kathleen Raine, a notable poet, illustrates the drift of some of the intelligentsia from the local chapel after the First World War

In loyalty to his father and his father's father, he had remained a Methodist and now instead of the sweet staid Sabbaths of Barington, my brother and I were led, he unwillingly but dutiful, I unwillingly and protesting, to the Cranbrook Wesleyan Methodist Church (it was not called a chapel, for the Cranbrook Park congregation had aspirations) every Sunday morning and evening. My father never doubted but in time he would by patience and his own unswerving conviction for what was right bring my mother to share his dearest beliefs and that I would, he took for granted . . . As for myself I detested the imprisoning hours I spent mentally re-arranging the panes in the stained-glass window, suggestive of the Victorian gothic style which had remotely influenced the design, taken no doubt from some builder's catalogue.

The congregation of shopkeepers and commercial travellers were no more my father's kind than they were of my mother's. He missed the warmth of that Methodism Coleridge so well described as a 'stove' ('heat without light') as he said; the revival meetings, the 'speaking with tongues', the simple faith but this he would never admit, for he, too, was trying to keep faith with a vanished past . . . he was a 'local preacher' as it was called and I heard him preach to these people often in his beautiful voice. On weeknights, he often spoke for the League of Nations. My father was a pacifist too.

Source: Kathleen Raine, *Farewell Happy Fields*, London: Hamish Hamilton, 1973; *The Land Unknown*, London: Hamish Hamilton, 1975, pp. 110–12.

67. *Conference and War 1915*

We are thankful that as a united people the Methodist Church from the first recognised the gravity of the issue and responded to the national call. We believe that the part that Britain is playing in this stupendous conflict has been directed by national honour, and not by selfish expediency.

We are fully convinced that it was morally impossible for a nation with our obligations and traditions to remain neutral while Belgium was being ravaged, France and Russia imperilled, and the gains of Christianity and civilisation jeopardised by a despotic ambition. Deeply as we deplore the appalling spectacle of bloodshed and widespread misery, we are driven to confess that 'a righteous war is better than an immoral peace' . . . Many have laid down their lives in this Great War against materialism and inhumanity. Although we keenly mourn their loss, we believe that by the shedding of their blood, they have done much to maintain the cause of truth and justice, progress and brotherhood . . . let us continue to pray and labour for the victory of right over wrong; of spiritual ideals over soul-degrading materialism, and for the ultimate advent of a worldwide and lasting peace founded upon law and righteousness which shall unite all nations in the service of humanity.

Source: Address to the Methodist Societies 1915. *Minutes of the Wesleyan Conference 1915*, pp. 453–6.

the fearful attrition of trench warfare. Many women, whose partners had died in war, were left unable to marry – their contribution to the wartime and post-war church must not be forgotten. The sociologist David Martin[5] said that liberal idealism either crusades for peace or treats war as a crusade. One can see in the twentieth century such swings in Methodism. The Conference Statement of 1915 can be compared with the pacifism of the 1930s, resistance to re-armament. Then later 'freedom fighters' were supported, with a move back to pacifist idealism when the 'freedom fighters' became dictators, which did not surprise some historians.

The approach to Methodist union[6]

John Scott Lidgett was President of the Wesleyan Conference in 1908. He was at the height of his theological acumen. Having set out his theology of Fatherhood and Christ as the Head of humanity in three major books, *The Spiritual Principle of the Atonement* (1897); *The Fatherhood of God* (1902); and *The Christian Religion, its Meaning and Proof* (1907), he set out an ecumenical agenda for the century in his presidential address.

68. *The future of church relations*

The unifying of Christendom for work in order to realize the Kingdom of God on earth is the primary object which faith sets before an enlightened Christian statesmanship. Where there are no differences our watchword must be union; where they are comparatively slight, federation; where they are more serious, yet not destructive of the fundamental agreement of Christianity co-operation in order to defend and promote the supreme interests and applications of our common Christian life. The schismatic is always a traitor. Most of all is he such in the present day. Methodism, if true to its original spirit will not look askance upon this great work or stand aloof from it.

Source: J. S. Lidgett, *Apostolic Ministry: Sermons and Addresses*, Culley, 1909, pp. 15–16.

Wesleyan initiatives for union began in 1913, resumed again after the war with leadership in the hands of Aldom French (1868–1962) firmly backed up by Sir Robert Perks. Six arguments were constantly used, stemming from Professor A. S. Peake, whose *Commentary* of 1919 had made him deservedly famous (see Box 69).

Not all were happy about this. There was a Wesleyan 'other side' led by J. E. Rattenbury of the West London Mission and Sir Henry Lunn who thought that Methodist union would actually hinder a wider union with the Church of England. Surely, the 'unionists' said, the Church of England would rather negotiate with one church than three. Rattenbury's argument was like that of Anglo-Catholics in the 1960s who felt that union with the Methodists would hinder relationships with the Roman Catholics. Some Wesleyans felt that the Primitive Methodists had no adequate view of the ordained ministry. Some Primitive Methodists believed the opposite, that the Wesleyans had an almost hierarchical view of ordained ministry, but Peake was able to show, by looking at recent Wesleyan statements, that this was no longer the case. Negotiations began seriously after 1918. Scott Lidgett, aided by Maldwyn Hughes, drew something

---

69. *Peake's six points for union*

1. He was convinced from his study of the *New Testament* that union was the Will of God. It was Christ's ideal for His church that it should be one both in spirit and in organisation. The *Letter to the Ephesians* was crucial.
2. *In the deeper loyalties they were one.* They had a common message, a common type of worship, an organisation with a fundamentally identical structure. It was always fatal for a church to coddle its denominationalisms.
3. *The taunts made by the outsider.* His seat on the commission conducted by the *Army and Religion* enquiry, had been an eye-opener. The men who faced the grim realities of life and death on the battlefields are in no mood to be patient with our sectarian spirit and they bid us set out house in order before we preach a League of Nations.
4. *The evangelisation of England* would receive a new impetus.
5. There was a movement in the direction of union in many departments of life – the *centripetal tendency* made it necessary that the three Methodist Churches should if possible combine their forces.
6. Methodist union was the first move towards the *Reunion of Christendom*.

Source: Leslie S. Peake, *Arthur Samuel Peake: A Memoir*, London: Hodder and Stoughton, 1930, pp. 162ff.

---

of the sting of the Wesleyan 'other side' by inserting in the final 1926 document this paragraph, which remained in the Deed of Union.

---

70. *Methodism's place in the Catholic Church of Christ*

The Methodist Church claims and cherishes its place in the Holy Catholic Church which is the Body of Christ. It rejoices in the inheritance of the Apostolic Faith, and loyalty accepts the fundamental principles of the historic Creeds and of the Protestant Reformation. It ever remembers that in the providence of God, Methodism was raised up to spread Scriptural holiness through the land by the proclamation of the evangelical faith and declares its unfaltering resolve to be true to its divinely appointed mission.

Source: *The Constitutional Practice and Discipline of the Methodist Church*, 5th ed., London: Methodist Publishing House, 1969, pp. 3, 288.

We must ask whether there was theological imprecision here or deliberate ambiguity. What, for instance, are the 'principles of the Protestant Reformation'? Calvinists would stress the sovereignty of God, the election of believers, the supremacy of Scripture and the 'final perseverance of believers'. Evangelical Arminians would stress, as did Lidgett, justification by faith, the completeness and all-sufficiency of our Lord's sacrifice and priesthood and the direct access of all believers to God through him, expressed as the priesthood of all believers. Peake would add the right of private judgement of the Scriptures.

Earlier in the negotiations, Peake had pleaded that Wesley's *Notes on the New Testament* should be dropped as part of the doctrinal standard for Methodist preachers as they were the work of an outmoded exegete, by which he meant the German Lutheran J. A. Bengel, who provided 40% of Wesley's work. He had even given the date of the second coming of Christ as 1836. Peake was probably right on this. It is, I dare to say, a piece of unnecessary eighteenth century baggage, which other churches in world Methodism find embarrassing at times. In the end the Deed of Union states:

---

71. *Doctrines*

The doctrines of the Evangelical Faith, which Methodism has held from the beginning, and still holds, are based upon the Divine revelation recorded in the Holy Scriptures. The Methodist Church acknowledges this revelation as the supreme rule of faith and practice. These evangelical doctrines to which the preachers of the Methodist Church, both Ministers and Laymen are pledged, are contained in Wesley's *Notes on the New Testament* and the first four volumes of his *Sermons*. The *Notes on the New Testament* and the 44 *Sermons* are not intended to impose any formal or speculative theology on Methodist Preachers but to set up standards of preaching and belief which should secure loyalty to the fundamental truths of the gospel of redemption and ensure the continual witness of the church, to the realities of the Christian experience of salvation.

Source: *The Constitutional Practice and Discipline of the Methodist Church*, 5th ed., London: Methodist Publishing House, 1969, pp. 3, 288.

This statement was acceptable to biblical scholars such as Peake for whom 'the divine revelation recorded in the Holy Scriptures' was vitally important. The doctrinal clauses were meant to embrace both conservative and liberal Methodists.

On the constitution, the Wesleyans were willing to abolish the 'Legal Hundred', as long as there was still a ministerial session of Conference. If ministers (or 'presbyters' as some prefer to call them now) are in any way an 'order', they would insist on some form of mutual consultation. The Wesleyans, too, were quite happy to have a Vice-President who must be a lay person (or now a Deacon) as long as the President or one of his predecessors would preside at ordinations. Primitive Methodists accepted this early on in the complex negotiations, which went on from 1918 to 1928. Few took seriously Sir Henry Lunn's

fear of a millionaire Lady Vice-President bullying the President!

There were still divisions on doctrine. The United Methodists were basically liberal, though the phrase in the Deed of Union about the sacraments being 'of divine institution and perpetual obligation' came from Alexander Kilham and the first MNC constitution. What of ministry? On this the Wesleyan 'other side' were undermined by the statement on the church of 1908, which provided the agreed clause which ran as follows:

---

72. *The Doctrine of the ministry*

Christ's ministers in the church are stewards in the household of God and shepherds of his flock. Some are called and ordained to this sole occupation, and have a principle and directing part in these great duties but they hold no priesthood differing in kind from that which is common to all the Lord's people and they have no exclusive title to the preaching of the gospel or the care of souls. These ministries are shared with them by others, to whom the Spirit divides his gifts severally as he wills. It is the universal conviction of the Methodist people that the office of the Christian Ministry depends upon the call of God who bestows the gift of the Spirit, the grace and the fruit, which indicate those whom he has chosen . . .

For the sake of church order and not because of any priestly virtue inherent in the office, the Ministers of the church are set apart by ordination to the Ministry of the Word and Sacraments.

Source: *The Constitutional Practice and Discipline of the Methodist Church*, 5th ed., London: Methodist Publishing House, 1969, pp. 4, 289.

From this statement, which does not define 'priesthood', it was logical of the new church to accept the principle and practice of lay presidency at the sacraments when ministers were not available, though Wesleyans had previously only allowed probationers to preside. It was made clear that Conference gave the authority for a lay person in a particular circuit – and only there – to preside, which is still the case. The ordained ministry is seen as representative. The old 'High Methodist' position had gone for ever. Even J. E. Rattenbury could not gainsay that. In 1928 the Wesleyan ministerial session of Conference accepted the scheme of 1926 by a vote of exactly 75%, a missionary arriving to vote at the last minute. It is significant that the smaller churches had agreed on union some time before and were becoming impatient with Wesleyan delay, although they had their opponents too who feared Wesleyan dominance. Certainly, in all the debates Scott Lidgett and Peake (who died in 1929) were 'the men of the match'. When the scheme was finally accepted, the Wesleyan New Testament scholar W. F. Howard (1880–1952) made clear the debt to Peake:

---

73. *W. F. Howard on A. S. Peake*

There are not a few on our side, who feared that the two smaller churches in their historical dislike of clericalism would hold in too light an esteem elements in our usage which our own experience has shown to be of the utmost value in the development of a strong and healthy churchmanship . . . If re-united Methodism holds up to the world its teaching about the body of Christ, the noble doctrine which Paul set forth in the *Epistle to the Ephesians*, we shall owe this move to Dr. Peake than to any other man.

Source: *Holborn Review*, 1930, p. 23.

In terms of statistics the united church of 1932 brought together 517,551 Wesleyans in Great Britain, 222,021 Primitive Methodists and 179,527 United Methodists. The ordained ministry consisted now of 2,510 Wesleyans, 1,131 Primitive Methodists and 729 United Methodists, with 18,785 Wesleyan local preachers, 12,896 Primitive Methodists and 5,232 United Methodists.

After Methodist union

When, in the presence of the Duke and Duchess of York (later King George VI and Queen Elizabeth) the Uniting Conference met in the Albert Hall on 20 September 1932, many had high hopes for the Methodist Church. It brought together 800,000 members – compared with 300,000 at the beginning of the twenty-first century. It is interesting to compare a parallel decline in the Church of Scotland, which had its re-union in 1929. Union was not the cause, though some sociologists have their views on that!

Within six months, Adolf Hitler had become Chancellor of the Third Reich. Who could foresee that by 1939 Great Britain would be at war with Germany? The challenge demanded by union in local areas often waited for solution until the period after the war, sometimes long after. The union, after long negotiation, was really 'top down'. At connexional level, due to astute businessmen behind the scenes, there was a smooth fusion of the colleges, schools and departments, even if it seemed, frankly, very like the Wesleyan style of management. But changes occurred too. *The Temperance and Social Welfare Department* led by Henry Carter and E. C. Urwin (1884–1978) moved away from obsession with drink and gambling to a very wide agenda of social concern, culminating in Carter's pioneering of what became *Christian Aid*. The Deed of Union, if somewhat vague, theologically did enable more conservative and more liberal thinkers and members to work together. Donald Soper could speak at Cliff College, Dinsdale Young (1861–1958) could preach with acceptance in his Conservative Evangelical style at the Central Hall, Westminster, with Leslie Weatherhead appearing at the City Temple in 1936. Both could speak from a 'generous orthodoxy' though with different emphases. Methodist groups such as the *Fellowship of the Kingdom* and the *School of Fellowship* were very different from the party exclusiveness which can still mar the Church of England. The theological colleges also catered for a great variety of candidates, many of whom developed a long relationship with tutors of the calibre of R. N. Flew, Maldwyn Hughes, Henry Bett, Wilbert Howard, Vincent Taylor and many more, who were part of a boom of Free Church scholarship.

But it was as if Methodism was really holding its breath after 1932. Scott Lidgett was President of the first Conference at the age of 78 with Sir Robert Perks, the first lay Vice-President, aged 84. Younger leaders took some time to achieve power. New drive and vigour was needed at both national and local level. Here is a sociologist's astute cynicism:

---

74. *Union – the reality*

Unionists were caught in a peculiar dilemma. On the one hand if union was to make Methodism a greater evangelical force throughout the country, the rationalization consequent upon closure of overlapping chapels was essential. On the other hand if they advocated closure of chapels as the main plank of their programme, the movement was doomed. They prevaricated . . . the purpose of union was to close the chapels, the price of union was to keep them open.

Source: R. Currie, *Methodism Divided*, London: Faber and Faber, 1968, pp. 177–8.

Apathy and snobbery were not unknown with a fear of ministerial domination on the Primitive Methodist side and a lack of development of lay pastoral care combining preaching, sacrament and financial support, which had become characteristic of some United Methodist churches, though they had many single-minister stations. Dr Eric Baker (1899–1973) implied, later, that the laity should not have voted 'yes' unless they had intended to consummate union locally.[7] The scheme lacked 'teeth'. 'Redundancy' had become a grim problem by the 1960s. In one Derbyshire mining village there were still three chapels in 1962 – full union in one building came about in 2004. The value of chapel life and community loyalty was underestimated at 'the

top'. It combined evangelical warmth, family loyalty and memories, intellectual and cultural life. It was not given up easily by those whose life was still very local.

Primitive Methodists felt the decay of village community in the agricultural and mining areas in the depression. They probably could not have survived on their own, although they had helped to produce a conciliatory style of trade unionism typified by Peter Lee (1864–1935) who gave his name later to a new town.

What did Methodism lose? From the Primitive Methodists a passion for free worship to balance a proper stress on worthy hymnody and an adequate liturgy. The *Methodist Hymn Book* of 1933 and the *Book of Offices* of 1936 were fine symbols of union. Also from the Primitive Methodists the role of the District Synod, which was at its best for them more than a business meeting with a great deal of participation. It had almost a diocesan pattern about it.

What of new styles to come? I was brought up in a

---

75. *Methodism*

When the World Methodist Conference met in Oxford in 1951, it was somehow symbolic that the patriarch of British Methodism, Scott Lidgett, now ninety-seven years old, should preach from the pulpit of the university church. He spoke for forty minutes and then collapsed into unconsciousness. Methodism had arrived. Was it about to pass away? The Methodism of these men [he features Flew, Weatherhead, Sangster, Soper, Rupp, Butterfield, Coulson – ministers and laymen] was as enlightened, mature, outgoing a form of Christianity as one might find anywhere, yet its problems of continued existence as a separate church were very considerable, even if a little masked by the modest religious revival, common to the whole nation, of those years.

Source: Adrian Hastings, *A History of English Christianity 1920–1985*, London: Collins, 1986, pp. 464–5.

Wolverhampton church built in 1926 in a new area. Our lay folk were from all the traditions. Everything could be new including fellowship, and house groups well in advance of their time. We had MAYC – evangelism by friendship – during the Second World War and there was a lively unsectarian Methodism to welcome one at college or university. Many ministers and lay leaders came from these new styles, seeing Methodism as a church of the future with a genuine contribution to the worship, theology and evangelism of a wider church in which many came to believe. Professor Adrian Hastings, a Roman Catholic, made some observations (see Box 75).

What can we learn from the consequence of union? We can see that if schemes are to be accepted, whether ecumenical or connexional (i.e. within Methodism) like the Covenant with the Church of England (accepted in 2003), or the 'Strategic Plan' of 'Our Calling' setting an agenda for Methodism, inspiration must come from 'below' as well as from 'above'. This need may not have been felt in 1932, but in our age of 'believing but not belonging' it is vital.

For discussion

1. Is there a Christian argument for a 'just war'?

2. Was it wise for so much support to be given to the Liberal Party? Should a church be neutral in politics? Why? Why not?

3. Are the arguments for church union used before 1932 valid for further unions?

4. Does the 'Deed of Union' still represent our theology?

5. Why did union of Methodist Connexions take so long to come about in some places?

Chronology 1900–1932

Wesleyanism	The Wider World
	1901 Death of Queen Victoria
1902 Death of Hugh Price Hughes	1902 End of Boer War
	1902 Balfour Education Act
1903 Cliff College	
1904 *Methodist Hymn Book*	1904–5 Welsh Revival
	1906 Liberal Election victory
1907 Union of MNC, UMFC and Bible Christians	
1908 Scott Lidgett, President	1908 Asquith, Prime Minister
	1910 Death of Edward VII
	1910 World Missionary Conference, Edinburgh
	1911 National Insurance
1918 Union Negotiations begin	1914–18 First World War
	1919 Treaty of Versailles
	1919 Federal Council of Free Churches
	1920 Fifth Lambeth Conference
	1920 Disestablishment of Church of Wales
1921 Opening of Wesley House, Cambridge	1921 International Missionary Conference
	1921 Irish Free State
	1924 COPEC Conference
	1924 First Labour Government
	1925 Life and Work – Stockholm
	1926 General Strike
	1927 Faith and Order – Lausanne
1928 Final Vote on Methodist union	1928 Missionary Conference – Jerusalem
1929 Methodist Church Union Act	1929 Presbyterian reunion in Scotland
	1929–31 Labour Party in power
	1930 Sixth Lambeth Conference
1932 Methodist union	1931–35 National Government under Macdonald

7

The Wesleyans and Other Christians

Evangelicals all

Recent writing on the Evangelical Revival uses a 'quadrilateral' suggested by Professor David Bebbington[1] to define who is an Evangelical:

- the stress on conversion, the belief that lives can be changed;
- biblicism, a particularly high regard for the authority of the Scriptures;
- a preaching of the cross, the sacrifice of Christ;
- activism, the expression of the gospel in action.

John Wesley would fit into that summary. His uniqueness (save for John Fletcher of Madeley) was his stress on the possibility of salvation for all, as opposed to predestination. This is 'the Arminianism of the heart'. There is, too, the necessity for growth through grace to perfect love of God and human beings. His contemporaries, 'the Calvinists of the heart' were concerned to assert the absoluteness of grace.

Here was a stress on predestination (not all would be saved) and a 'final perseverance' (once saved, always saved). George Whitefield, who saw the world as his parish, believed that preaching was the means God used to save his elect, a matter which Wesley saw as a means of saving all who responded. Humanity was, for him, free to say 'No' and could

fall away. This led to a split in the evangelical camp with most Church of England Evangelicals taking a moderately Calvinist approach. Charles Simeon (1759–1836), curate-in-charge of Holy Trinity Church, Cambridge, whose influence was immense, met the aged Wesley, seeking to 'dumb down' this particular divergence (see Box 77).

It is not possible to understand the movement for world mission without noting the way in which moderate Calvinist and Arminian were producing a style where agreements were more important than arguments. Yet Evangelicals still tended to demand that Methodists leave them to run their parishes despite the problems of pastoral continuity – one Evangelical might not follow another in a parish. This led to the Simeon Trust of 1817 and the Pastoral Aid Society of 1836 to ensure Evangelical succession. It had the effect of hardening party lines

---

76. *John Newton – from slavery to freedom*

Amazing grace (how sweet the sound)
That saved a wretch like me!
I once was lost but now am found,
Was blind but now I see.
. . . God's grace has brought me safe thus far,
And he will lead me home.

Source: Olney Hymns 1779, HP 215.

---

77. *Young Simeon and the elderly Wesley seek peace 1784*

Then, Sir, with your leave, I will put up my dagger again for this is all my Calvinism – this is my salvation, my justification, my final perseverance; it is in substance all that I hold and as I hold it, and if you please, instead of searching out terms and phrases to be a ground of contention between us, we will cordially unite in all things wherein we agree.

Source: Preface to Simeon's *Horae Homileticae* cited in H. C. G. Moule, *Charles Simeon*, London: IVF, 1948, p. 100.

---

since the high churchmen set up the Additional Curates' Society in 1837, with a similar purpose. Evangelical Anglicans, too, clearly had a strong attachment to the Protestantism of the national church, to the Thirty Nine Articles, the Prayer Book and the Bible with a stress on justification by faith and a firm belief that the primary task of the church was mission and evangelism which spilled over into the world mission of the *Church Missionary Society* (1799) which followed up the *Baptist Missionary Society* of 1792 and the *London Missionary Society* of 1795, which proposed but failed to achieve a genuine ecumenism. Simeon, if willing to 'put up his sword', did not wish to see the clergyman beating the bush and the dissenters snatching the game. He stood for the parish system and the expansion of Anglicanism overseas.

The interdenominational movement in the 1790s, not least in Sunday Schools, was followed by a growing denominational integrity, which persisted throughout the next century. But there were areas where Wesleyans could heartily co-operate. As we have seen, this was so in the battle against slavery. Evangelicals accepted much of the moral philosophy of the day. There was, too, a fortuitous combining of political and moral elements. Wesleyans such as Joseph Butterworth (1770–1826) and Thomas Thompson (1754–1828), both members of Parliament, supported William Wilberforce and the

'Clapham Sect' of Evangelicals in the Church of England as, of course, did Richard Watson. In 1817, Zachary Macaulay, a leading abolitionist, wrote to Hannah More stating that 'Watson, the Wesleyan Methodist, spoke with singular delicacy and feeling with a degree of good taste which would have done credit to such a man as Reginald Heber. He is certainly an able and honest man.' That was slightly patronising. As we have seen, Watson later supported T. B. Macaulay in a parliamentary election against the factory reformer Michael Sadler who had Methodist roots – though Bunting did not support Thornton, another abolitionist – part of the complex game of politics!

Other areas of co-operation included the distribution of Christian literature. Methodism used tracts before the *Religious Tract Society* (1799). The *Wesleyan Tract Society*, reformed in 1828 by Conference, produced 36,787,111 tracts between 1825 and 1838. The Religious Tract Society was interdenominational from the start. The tracts did reach some of the poor as a response to the more radical tracts of the time. Legh Richmond's *The Dairyman's Daughter* and *The Sinners' Friend* were immensely popular. Some of this matter might seem patronising now, although Hannah More, the great Anglican pamphleteer, has recently been shown to

---

78. *Possibility of missionary ecumenism, 9 May 1796*

It is declared to be a fundamental principle of the Missionary Society that our design is not to send Presbyterianism, Independency, Episcopacy or any other form of church order and government (about which there may be differences among serious persons) but the glorious gospel of the Blessed God to the heathen; and that it shall be left (as it even ought to be left) to the minds of the persons whom God shall call into the Fellowship of His son among them to assume for themselves such form of church government as shall appear most agreeable to the Word of God.

Source: R. Lovett, *History of the London Missionary Society, 1795–1895*, London, 1899, p. 49.

---

have been less concerned with keeping people in their proper station than once seemed the case.

Methodism had its own Bible distribution arm in the *Navy and Army Bible Society*, sponsored by two Wesleyan laymen, John Davies and George Cussons, in 1779 with the aid of John Thornton of Clapham, and supported by both archbishops. Much bigger was the *British and Foreign Bible Society* (1801), supported by the Clapham Group. The Wesleyan scholar Adam Clarke was at one time loaned to the society to use his immense linguistic skill, a happy relationship which was to foreshadow the long co-operation between Anglicans, Methodists and other Nonconformists in biblical scholarship. Here, in publishing, was one factor in what has been called 'the battle for the hearts' producing the vibrant religion of the nineteenth century, not least among the working class though we must not exaggerate, and forget that 30% of the population was still illiterate. The magazines of the time such as the *Wesleyan Methodist Magazine* (formerly the *Arminian Magazine*) also propagated a style of morality which seems rather stern, frowning on romantic novels, dancing, balls and card playing. Wilberforce saw great scope for co-operation in reforming manners and behaviour.

---

79. *Wilberforce's Catholic spirit 1798*

Let them cultivate a Catholic spirit of universal goodwill and amiable fellowship towards all those of whatever sect or denomination who differing from them in non-essentials agree with them in the grand fundamentals of Religion. Let them countenance men of real piety, wherever they are found; and encourage in others every attempt to repress the progress of vice and receive and diffuse the influence of Religion and virtue.

Source: W. Wilberforce, *A Practical View of the Prevailing Religious System of Professed Christians in the Higher and Middle Classes in the country Contrasted with real Christianity*, 1798 (Ancient and Modern Library of Theological Literature, London, n.d., p. 256).

Ford Brown[2] was rather harsh in claiming that Wilberforce adopted the impossible task of seeking to reform the morals and manners of a society, while disturbing no element of its socially immoral structure, Evangelical discipline and responsibility before the great taskmaster's eye could be secularised as respectability, but it must not be underestimated.

There was later considerable Wesleyan interest in the *Evangelical Alliance* of 1846,[3] of which Jabez Bunting and later William M. Bunting, his son, were Honorary Secretaries. It is quite likely that W. M. Bunting (1805–66) was the first non-Anglican to lead prayers in Lambeth Palace, when the Archbishop of Canterbury (J. B. Sumner, an Evangelical) met those concerned with the Alliance. The Alliance's doctrinal statement – not, it was made clear, a creed – made the 'frontier' clear enough (see Box 80).

While clearly the Alliance was greatly concerned with study, prayer (e.g. the Universal Week of Prayer in January), liberty and world mission, there was an anti-high church and anti-Catholic element here which would be supported by some Wesleyans (the Buntings, William Arthur and later Sir William McArthur (Lord Mayor of London) and H. H. Fowler). It was John Angell James the Evangelical Congregationalist who saw it, a trifle foolishly, as opposing 'the three Ps – Popery, Puseyism and Plymouth Brethrenism'. Later the Alliance was concerned with Darwinism and the dangers of new forms of theology such as *Essays and Reviews* which was published a year after Darwin's *The Origin of Species* (1859). Thomas Jackson, the Wesleyan, found the *Essays and Reviews* 'mischievous and revolting'. There was also a streak of pre-millenarianism (expectancy of the second coming of Christ) among some evangelicals, which alienated younger Wesleyans like Hugh Price Hughes and Scott Lidgett. Hughes called the Alliance 'a fortuitous concourse of Evangelical individuals who meet together occasionally to say that they love one another'. The plenary inspiration of Scripture was another sticking point. Recent scholarship has been rather more positive on the Alliance, but Dr Clyde Binfield saw the YMCA, founded in 1844,

80. *The Evangelical Alliance 1846*

The Parties composing the Alliance shall be such persons only as hold and maintain what are usually understood to be evangelical views, in regard to the matter of doctrine understood, namely:

1. The divine Inspiration, Authority and Sufficiency of the Holy Scriptures.
2. The Right and Duty of Private Judgment in the Interpretation of the Holy Scriptures.
3. The Unity of the Godhead over the Trinity of Persons therein.
4. The utter Depravity of Human Nature, in consequences of the Fall.
5 The Incarnation of the Son of God, His work of Atonement for sinners of mankind and His mediatorial Intercession and Reign.
6. The Justification of the sinner by faith alone.
7. The work of the Holy Spirit in Conversion and Sanctification of the sinner.
8. The immortality of the Soul, the Resurrection of the Body, the Judgment of the World by our Lord Jesus Christ with the Eternal Blessedness of the Righteous, and the Eternal Punishment of the Wicked.
9. The divine Institution of the Christian Ministry and the obligation and perpetuity of the Ordinance of Baptism and the Lord's Supper.

Source: I. Randall and D. Hilborn, *One Body in Christ: the History and Significance of the Evangelical Alliance*, Carlisle: Paternoster, 2001, pp. 358–9.

as an ecumenical portent, while the Alliance 'did not possess the vital influence to be expected from the nineteenth century Evangelical Revival's only ecumenical movement'.[4] In the next century Samuel Chadwick became a notable Wesleyan supporter. The Alliance is now far more congenial to some Methodists. We can summarise this section by stating that Wesleyanism was in danger in the mid-nineteenth century of theological isolation, while, later, some Evangelicals in the Church of England began to feel that Methodism could become dangerously liberal.

The Catholic revival in Anglicanism and the Wesleyans

Recently, Dr Peter Nockles[5] has shown how strong and important the high churchmen were in the eighteenth and early nineteenth century. As far as Methodism is concerned, they rarely explored Wesley's thinking – Alexander Knox (1757–1831) was an exception. He saw Methodism as 'that spiritual view of religion which implies an habitual devotedness to God 'and Wesley as a link between Protestant and Catholic spirituality'. High churchmen began the exaltation of episcopacy as the sine qua non of church order, which was taken up by the Oxford Movement led by J. H. Newman, E. B. Pusey and J. Keble in 1833. Bishop Horsley of Rochester certainly saw Wesleyanism as dangerous. Thomas Sikes, of the same school, called Wesley 'that saucy itinerant', and also condemned 'occasional conformity' (whereby some Methodists received Holy Communion in the parish churches) as 'disgraceful and indefensible'. The so-called 'Hackney Phalanx' of high churchmen (named after H. H. Norris, Rector of North Hackney, and Joshua Watson, a London wine merchant, whose brother was Rector of Hackney) was extremely important in pioneering church day schools, which were the means of educating thousands of the children of the poor, but which, as we have seen, caused division in many parishes up to and including the Education Act of 1902 and its sequels.

The tragedy of this period of religious life is that Wesleyans and Evangelicals, high churchmen and Oxford Movement men never realised what godly heritage they had in common from a diverse and rich Anglican tradition. The parties drifted into isolation and cantankerousness that for long frustrated some of the impact they might have had on society. It was not the Oxford Movement alone which pushed the Wesleyans into the Free Church camp. A threatened but increasingly resurgent Anglicanism clashed socially, politically and theologically with a Wesleyanism past its peak of membership in relation to population by 1840.

With the history of the Oxford or Anglo-Catholic Movement we cannot here be concerned, but only with its influence on Wesleyanism.[6] The Movement was first intended by its leaders to stress holiness and authority rather than ceremonial or ritual which came later. The desire to find a solid authority for the church other than power given by the state led to a stress on tradition and the 'Apostolic Succession' of bishops marking off churches which could stress their links with the early church. This meant the 'unchurching' of other denominations including not only British nonconformist churches and Methodism but also Lutheran and Reformed churches. The Wesleyans, having in many ways supported the Church of England, could only feel isolated and even betrayed. The *Tracts for the Times* (hence the name 'Tractarian' used of the Oxford men) written from 1833 onwards were replied to by some leading Wesleyans including George Osborn, Alfred Barrett and Dr John Hannah (1792–1867) paralleling work by Thomas Jackson. When Pusey wrote on Wesleyanism protesting that it believed in 'salvation by feeling', he was, no doubt, referring to contemporary revivalism rather than Wesley. Jackson, in reply, pitted the best of Wesley and Wesleyan thought against Pusey, who did not reply. On apostolic succession

---

81. *Thomas Jackson on the real Apostolic Succession*

There is . . . an Apostolic Succession . . . in which every minister should be careful to stand, or he will be found an intruder into the sacred office . . . the true Apostolic Succession is a succession to a ministry which is characterised by Apostolic truth, by Apostolic zeal and faithfulness, by Apostolic efficiency and power, by Apostolic labour and self-denial and by Apostolic success. In this succession we believe that our fathers stood and we ourselves are in it as far as we are actuated by the same Spirit and tread in their steps.

Source: T. Jackson, *Wesleyan Methodism, a Revival of Apostolic Christianity*, London, 1839, p. 35; cf. *A Letter to the Rev. E. B. Pusey*, 1842.

Jackson made no bones about its meaning for him.

Soon, both the high churchmen and the Evangelicals were caught up in a demand for a more professional style of parish clergyman[7] – upright, zealous, a capable preacher, pastor and organiser with a multiplicity of meetings in the parish – and in the case of the High churchmen a concentration on the Eucharist. Evangelicals, too, often shared a new stress on the sacraments with more frequent Holy Communion, though in a different style. With a lack of liturgical knowledge this led the 'ritualists' to borrow from contemporary Catholicism and from the romanticism of architects like Pugin, the reviver of the 'gothic' style of architecture which spread across the churches including the Wesleyans as we have seen. There was a return to a romantic pre-Reformation Middle Ages. But the great discovery of the Oxford Movement was that the church was a living organism, a matter on which two Methodist theologians, William Burt Pope and Benjamin Gregory (1820–1900) in his fine Fernley lecture *The Holy Catholic Church* (1873), began to produce a genuine Wesleyan ecclesiology.

The tragedy was that the Tractarians were fundamentally Arminian as were the Wesleyans, deriving much of their spirituality and desire for holiness from many of the same sources from which Wesley had drawn so freely. At the end of the century some Anglo-Catholics realised this. There was also, stemming from reforms by Prime Minister Peel and Bishop Blomfield (the Anglican Bunting), a renewal of the Church of England in many a parish, with a tremendous number of new churches. In Leeds, for instance, the Church of England began to compete with the Wesleyans. In the diocese of Lincoln, Bishop Kaye had 200 parsonages built or made habitable. In the diocese of Oxford, livings were increased from 356 to 630.[8]

The Tractarians stressed the need for awe, reserve and mystical awareness rather than the subjective feelings which dominated revivalism. So Pusey continued to deplore Wesleyanism, which for him threatened to be one of the most dreadful scourges with which the church was ever afflicted, the great antagonist of penitence. Tragically, Pusey was a superb preacher of the cross but could not see that the response to it might not be hidden but expressed with a trumpet voice. The notable Danish theologian N. F. S. Grundtvig made the point about the tragedy of it all.

---

82. *The irony of division*

Could these two movements find each other and coalesce, could they, at the same time, have their eyes opened for the importance of the word of faith in the Christian congregation, then the conditions of a rich church life would be in existence in England.

Source: N. F. S. Grundtvig, *A Letter to the Press When Visiting Oxford in December 1843.*

The consequence was antagonism between Wesleyanism and the Church of England, which was very different from the view of Thomas Jackson as late as 1834 that 'the country cannot do without an Establishment either in resisting Popery, socinianism and infidelity or in the maintenance of Christian holiness and virtue'. Now there was a coldness and renewed fear of Popery. J. H. Rigg, at this time in a very anti-Anglican phase, saw no possibility or desire for union with the Church of England. He was rather eager to show that Wesley after 1738 had

---

83. *Punch – Conference in a naughty mood 1868*

You offer one hand to the Papal band
And the other to us extend.
Can you really hope that we and the Pope
Can acknowledge a mutual friend?
You tell us your bark is not an ark.
We don't believe that's true.
We'd trust a raft before your craft
Just paddle your own canoe.

Source: A. L. Drummond, *The Churches Pictured by 'Punch'*, London: Epworth Press, 1947, p. 13; W. H. Mackintosh, *Disestablishment and Liberation*, London: Epworth Press, 1972, pp. 186–7.

---

thrown off 'the rags of popery' and 'the grave clothes of superstition' which was very much his own 'spin' on Wesley's thinking.

In 1868, Pusey, disillusioned about any rapprochement with the Roman Catholics, wrote to the Wesleyan Conference in a new irenic tone. The President of Conference said that the Wesleyans were in a midway position between the Establishment and Dissent. But, rather naughtily, elements in Conference moved further, expressing Rigg's view in a poem.

The same Year *Punch* had a cartoon showing Dr Pusey dressed in cassock, gown and bands inviting a demure and obviously Wesleyan lady to accompany him to church. She politely declines. Above her is a portrait of John Wesley clad in similar fashion to Pusey. We can sum up this period with a

---

84. *Benjamin Hellier on reunion*

In the first instance the Church of England was a house divided against itself.

The two Convocations and the high-church party would never reach a common mind.

Second, the Methodist Conference would likewise never reach a common mind on re-union.

Third, the mind of both churches would not arrive at a common policy even if they could agree among themselves.

Fourthly, if the Convocation and the Conference did reach common mind, their suggestions would prove unacceptable to the Methodist people as a while.

Finally, even if the first four points were met, the sanction of Parliament would be withheld.

These things considered and without saying what may or may not be possible one hundred years hence when you and I shall no longer be dwelling on this earth, we may say that the question of organic union between the Methodists and the Church of England is one which belongs to the region of pure speculation and as a question on which practical men can take no action, if has not yet come within the field of vision.

Source: *Benjamin Hellier: His Life and Teaching*, London, 1889, pp. 134–5.

statement by Benjamin Hellier, Tutor at Headingley College, Leeds, who gives reasons why the union of the Church of England and Wesleyanism was impracticable, a statement the irony of which will not escape readers.

'Olive branches from a catapult' is how Dr John Newton describes other moves from Bishop Wordsworth of Lincoln in 1873. After that, there were mere flurries until the scholars began to join together in Bible translations and biblical thinking. Other groups, such as the YMCA, and the great support from some surprising quarters for the Moody and Sankey Missions and growing work among students which was to flower into the *Student Christian Movement*, were streams which could flow into a growing desire for more co-operation between Christians especially on the mission field overseas, which was at the height of its great century.

New initiatives in ecumenism

Earlier historians such as G. M. Trevelyan and Sir Ernest Barker saw the interaction between the Church of England and Nonconformity as the central factor in English political life for two centuries, producing the two-party systems of Whigs and Tories, Liberals and Conservatives. This was still the case in Victorian times, but it was beginning to become far less easy to define as a new century dawned. Liberalism had split over Irish Home Rule, as indeed had the Wesleyans over that issue both in Ireland and England, though the Methodist Church, when the final break away of the Republic came, was able to work on both sides of the new frontier. Anglicans produced the Chicago–Lambeth Quadrilateral as a doctrinal model, and a necessity in any final union with other churches.

The fourth side of the Quadrilateral was the hinge on which the door swung open or remained shut – was it to be demanded before any scheme can be formulated, or the goal after union had been agreed, as was the case in South India in 1947? The Anglicans were now more willing to have relation-

---

> **85.** *The Lambeth Quadrilateral*
>
> 1. The *Holy Scriptures* of the Old and New Testament as 'containing all things necessary to salvation' and as being the rule and ultimate standard of faith.
> 2. The *Apostles' Creed* as the Baptismal Symbol and the *Nicene Creed* as the sufficient statement of the Christian faith.
> 3. The *two sacraments* instituted by Christ Himself – Baptism and the Supper of the Lord – ministered with unfailing use of Christ's words of institution and the elements ordained by Him.
> 4. The *Historic Episcopate*, locally adapted in the methods of its administration to the varying needs of the nations and peoples called of God into the unity of His Church.
>
> *Source*: R. Rouse and S. C. Neill (eds), *A History of the Ecumenical Movement 1517–1948*, London: SPCK, 1967, p. 265.

---

ships with Free Church people, especially when the education debates began to die down with the acceptance by the Free Churches, albeit for many unwillingly, of the dual system. New initiatives include the *Review of the Churches* from 1891 onwards in which Sir Percy Bunting (1830–1911), Jabez Bunting's grandson, played a major part with Henry Lunn. Lunn, in his capacity as travel agent, initiated the constructive and creative Grindelwald Conference from 1891 to 1896, which brought together, in a Swiss environment, leaders who had never ever sat together, let alone prayed together.

The Free Churches began to seek new forms of unity in which, following the first Free Church Congress of 1892, Hugh Price Hughes was prominent.[9] Some Free churchmen, like the polemical Silvester Horne, Congregationalist, saw the Free Churches as united against Popery, Puseyism, Establishment dominance and all that. Hughes was more positive. He was the first President of the *National Council of Evangelical Free Churches*, elected on a representative basis. Box 86 shows Hughes' statement.

This viewpoint excluded the Unitarians and the

Salvation Army, but it was not entirely political or social. There was the Free Church Catechism of 1898 – criticised by the conservative Wesleyan Marshall Randles (1826–1904). This was followed by the *Simultaneous Mission to London* in 1901, and missions elsewhere led by the Wesleyan evangelist Gipsy Smith. Smith played a leading part in the Welsh Revival of 1904–5, which, though short-lived, brought many into the chapels, though in Newtown it had no apparent influence on Wesleyanism. Revival and political agitation seemed to go together. The Council divided on the Boer War. The acumen of Scott Lidgett was needed to prevent the Council forgetting its spirituality in favour of attempting to dominate the Liberal Party.

The World War saw much greater co-operation through chaplaincies. The Baptist J. H. Shakespeare

---

86. *Free Church unity 1896*

So long as any public question divides us and is calculated to destroy our internal unity; it would be suicidal for us to touch it. But there are good causes such as the Temperance Movement, the Purity Movement, the Anti-gambling Movement and the 'Peace Movement' which, although they have their political sides are especially moral and Christian and which, without fear of internal discord we must promote with all our might . . . I believe that our future and the future of the British Empire and therefore to a great extent the future of the human race depends under God on the extent to which the churches we represent are able to distinguish between denominational loyalty and bigotry, between denominational independence and sectarianism, between denominational activity and schism. Can we rise above small ideals and narrow ambitions? . . . We are not one in the Pope. We are not one in the Crown but we are one in Christ . . . in the most important and influential quarter of the globe we can decisively influence the course of human events. We can greatly hasten the advent of the blissful day.

Source: Proceedings of the National Council of the Evangelical Free Churches, 1896, Presidential Address, pp. 24–38.

---

87. *The Lambeth Appeal to All Christian People 1920*

We acknowledge all those who believe in our Lord Jesus Christ, and have been baptized into the name of the Holy Trinity, as sharing with us membership in the universal Church of Christ which is His Body . . . The vision which rises before us is that of a church, genuinely Catholic, loyal to all Truth, and gathering into its fellowship all 'who profess and call themselves Christians' . . . May we not reasonably claim that the Episcopate is the one means of providing such a ministry [i.e. acknowledged by every part of the church] . . . It is not that we call in question for a moment the spiritual reality of the ministries of those Communions which do not possess the Episcopate. On the contrary, we thankfully acknowledge that these ministries have been manifestly blessed and owned by the Holy Spirit as effective means of grace. But we submit that considerations alike of history and of present experience justify the claim we make on behalf of the Episcopate. [Episcopal ordination is then to be the norm but 'in so acting (that is accepting episcopacy) no one of us could possibly be taken to repudiate his past ministry'.]

Source: G. K. A. Bell (ed.), Documents on Christian Unity, 1920–4, London: Oxford University Press, 1924, pp. 1–6.

(1857–1928) advocated Free Church federation and ultimate union as a stage to corporate reunion with the Church of England. The Wesleyan J. H. Moulton saw federation as a reasonable goal, what P. T. Forsyth called 'the United States of the Church'. One result was the *Federal Council of the Evangelical Free Churches*, inaugurated in 1919, without at first Wesleyan support. That took place in 1920, with the inevitable Scott Lidgett as Moderator in 1923. The two Councils united in 1940 as the *Free Church Federal Council*, now the Free Church Group in Churches together in England. The 1919 body was able to respond to the Lambeth Conference of Anglican bishops held in 1920.

Scott Lidgett, with great optimism, saw this Appeal as the most important statement from the

Church of England on church unity since the Reformation. He played a full part in the Wesleyan reply of July 1922, which accepted three sides of the quadrilateral.

When an Anglican 'Memorandum' of 1923 made clear that the ministries of non-episcopalian churches were used of the Spirit 'within their several spheres', it appeared to take away with one hand what they had granted with the other. In 1925 this was further clarified, and for the Free Churches, strongly represented by Maldwyn Hughes and Scott Lidgett from the Wesleyans, was the virtual end of negotiations for a time – indeed the Presbyterian Carnegie

---

88. *The Wesleyan reply to Lambeth July 1922*

We are bound to state . . . our fundamental conviction that neither in our Lord's own teaching, nor in any part of the New Testament is one form of church polity prescribed as essential to the church; and that no particular form of ministry can claim 'the direct commission of Christ', or of the Apostles, as giving to it an authority to which no others are entitled . . .

a) The proposal to make episcopal ordination an essential part of the scheme of union, if it be interpreted as implying re-ordination could not be accepted by those who believe themselves to be already ministers in the Church of God . . . we could not under any circumstances consent to limit the freedom of fellowship which we already enjoy with non-episcopal churches.

b) The difficulties raised by a connexion between church and state form an important consideration . . .

f) We feel it necessary to affirm the adherence of the Wesleyan Methodist Church to the principles of the Protestant Reformation.

Source: G. K. A. Bell, *Documents on Christian Unity*, 1920-4, London: Oxford University Press, 1924, pp. 110–15; *Minutes* 1922.

Simpson, jokingly, said that if he had to take up episcopacy, it might be safer to take it from the Pope.

Much more positive was the ecumenism stemming from the worldwide Christian Movement coalescing in the Student Christian Movement and the Missionary Conference at Edinburgh in 1910, often seen as the real beginning of modern ecumenism. It was presided over by an American Methodist, John R. Mott (1865–1955), and followed by world conferences on *Faith and Order* at Lausanne in 1927 and on *Life and Work* at Stockholm in 1928, which were presages of what became the World Council of Churches, set up finally in 1948 after the Second World War. W. F. Lofthouse, Sir Henry Lunn and Luke Wiseman were on the continuation committee appointed at Lausanne; Lofthouse presented several Methodist statements of importance at this time, in the end strongly supporting moves towards the Church of South India which was inaugurated in 1947.[10]

For discussion

1. How would you define an Evangelical?

2. Are we nearer to Anglican Evangelicals than to other parties within the Anglican Communion?

3. What does the Ecumenical Movement mean now?

4. Should British Methodism embrace episcopacy? Why? Why not?

5. How does co-operation between the churches work in your area?

Conclusion:
What Can We Learn
from the Wesleyans?

The historian Eric Hobsbawm reminds us that for many the historical memory is no longer alive:

> The destruction of the past or rather of the social mechanisms that link contemporary experience to that of earlier generations is one of the most characteristic and eerie phenomena of the late twentieth century. Most young men and women at the century's end grew up in a sort of permanent present lacking any organic relation to the public past and the times we live in. This makes historians, whose business is to remember what others forget, more essential at the end of the second millennium than ever before.[1]

A few years later this is even more the case. What can Jabez Bunting and his opponents possibly mean to those in the Methodist Church now, let alone those searching for spirituality outside any church? Yet the TV 'history industry' shows the other side of people's interest in history with its inevitable simplifications. Have we passed from being concerned with denominational loyalty and the 'ecumenism of time' to the task of being the church in situations very different from Victorian days? Then, suddenly, we find ourselves making the same mistakes as our forbears. So I shall suggest four

areas where we can learn from the experiences of the Wesleyans.

Connexion

John Wesley had a clear idea of a 'connexion'.[2] It was a number of local societies which had agreed to unite themselves in a common bond of discipline with a code of regulations and a body of agreed doctrine. It was neither sect nor denomination. He was able to combine pragmatism – 'following the blow', as he put it, with discipline, evangelism and revivalism with spiritual growth and control. This meant that the itinerant preacher was under his strict control – and if they did not accept that they could go elsewhere to serve God. After his death, there was a constant tension between connexionalism and local initiatives, sometimes dealt with in an immature dictatorial manner, even with the best of motives.

What now? Let us take two examples. Ministers (presbyters) are 'received into full connexion' and ordained at the Conference, not locally. They are appointed by the Conference, through the Stationing Committee, even if district and local options are carefully noted. There is still a feel of availability to the Connexion, which was at the heart of Wesleyanism, not least in its world missionary movement. The minister was, and is, appointed to a circuit not to a local church. This is in contrast to other Free Church styles. The weakness of Wesleyanism was that pragmatism hardened and 'froze' so that the rule continued that ministers should move every three years. The concept behind this was not ridiculous; the minister was not the 'servant' of local groups but represented the whole church. Originally, it enabled young men not to bore people! Is that still relevant? A local preacher is trained in a particular circuit but on a connexional pattern. He or she serves the circuit, which secures a variety of preaching. Clearly some now, especially Evangelicals, would prefer to sustain a particular style. The connexional way seeks to avoid a party line. A team of preachers can share their insights, assisting each other and using varied abilities, strengths and theological insights. A local preacher when 'fully accredited' is able to use his or her gifts anywhere in the church, as is a church member whose membership, symbolised by the annual ticket (it was quarterly in earlier days) can be transferred and welcomed anywhere. This is still a normative feature.

We can also point to the way in which the 'strong' can help the 'weak' so that small rural societies can be supported by more affluent churches. When I visited my home church, with its 400 members, I commented on the very large collection. 'Ah yes,' said the Treasurer, 'we support a church and its minister in the inner belt of the city in all their community activities.' *That* is the connexion in action. Other churches might learn from it. The task is still that which faced the Wesleyans – how to combine the connexional with its stress on the national and the international with what we now call 'subsidiarity' or local initiative. The Wesleyans so often failed here through Conference arrogance and local desire for independence. Can Methodism learn from their mistakes?

Inclusivity

The Evangelical Arminian tradition that God's grace is for all, and indeed in all, should enable Methodism to combine what can be called a generous orthodoxy with a concern for the inclusive nature of the church. Scripture can still be central, illuminated by the whole of Christian tradition, confirmed by the disciplined use of reason and verified in personal experience. Methodism can avoid a wooden biblicism, the dead hand of overstress on tradition (even Wesleyan traditions) and too much reliance on either the intellect or the emotions. This can mean groups stressing different emphases but belonging together and avoiding party strife. Cliff College and the Urban Theology Unit can share an 'optimism of grace' which can link conservative and radical.

Worship

The Wesleyans had a great variety of worship styles combining the use of responsive forms with considerable freedom, even if some feared that revivalism could get out of hand. Can Methodism still share its style of hymnody with other churches or are we the last generation to love, sing and imbibe theology from Charles Wesley's hymns? Methodism still has, unlike other churches an official hymn book. Is this now an outmoded style? Can we still cultivate a 'both . . . and' emphasis in our corporate worship with preaching still having a feel of the open-air evangelism which was the case in Wesleyanism – the offer of Christ to people?

Lay participation

Wesleyans had to learn, sometimes with agony, the absolute need for lay participation at every level of the church's life. 'The priesthood of all believers' does not imply that everyone can do everybody else's

Spirit-given task, rather it means that each has the privilege of offering service, sacrifice and prayer, the living out of the faith. Evangelism and concern for

---

89. *From Wesley to our day*

Allowing for the lapse of two hundred years, there is a close correspondence between the classic ecumenical movement with the profile of John Wesley that informed Methodists and others could recognize. Wesley's vision, programme and praxis were marked by the following six principal features. First, he looked to the *Scriptures* as the primary and abiding testimony to the redemptive work of God in Christ. Second, he was utterly committed to the ministry of *evangelism*, where the gospel was to be preached to every creature and needed only to be accepted by faith. Third, he valued with respect to the Christian tradition and the doctrine of the church, a *generous orthodoxy*, wherein theological opinions might vary as long as they were consistent with the apostolic teaching. Fourth, he expected *sanctification* to show itself in the moral earnestness and loving deeds of the believers. Fifth, he manifested and encouraged a *social concern* that was directed toward the neediest of neighbours. Sixth, he found in the *Lord's Supper* a sacramental sign of the fellowship graciously bestowed on the part of those who will glorify God and enjoy Him forever. These are the features which must be strengthened in contemporary Methodism, if we are to maintain our historic identity, speak with a significant voice on the ecumenical scene and keep on a recognizably Christian track as the ways diverge.

Source: Geoffrey Wainwright, *Methodists in Dialogue*, Nashville: Abingdon Press, 1995, pp. 283–4.

---

the community, in particular the poor, cannot be the sole business of the ordained or full-time lay worker. The Wesleyans could sometimes appear complacent, but, in the end, burst out of self-reliance with the NCH, the Central Halls and later a concern for the service of youth by the evangelism of friendship. The lack of lay leaders is now a desperate need. We end with a statement about the Wesleyan tradition, using the phrase in the broadest sense (Box 89).

For discussion

1. Do we live in a world for younger people without history? Do our traditions matter any more?

2. Does the idea of the church as a 'connexion' appeal to you, or should it all be local?

3. Do the hymns of Charles Wesley still get sung in your church? Do younger people find them meaningful?

4. Some think that Methodist theology is defined by scripture, tradition, reason and experience. Does that 'ring a bell' with you? Which is most important in defining what we believe?

5. Are Geoffrey Wainwright's six points still valid? Which is the most important for you or your church?

6. Do you think Methodism has a future in Great Britain?

Notes

Introduction

For John Wesley the standard biography is H. D. Rack, *Reasonable Enthusiast: John Wesley and the Rise of Methodism*, 3rd ed., London: Epworth Press, 2002; also R. P. Heitzenrater, *Wesley and the People Called Methodists*, Nashville: Abingdon Press, 1995; J. M. Turner, *John Wesley, the Evangelical Revival and the Rise of Methodism in England*, London: Epworth Press, 2002; a more radical view can be found in J. Kent, *Wesley and the Wesleyans*, Cambridge: Cambridge University Press, 2002.

1. T. B. Macaulay, *Critical and Historical Essays*, London, 1866, vol. 2, pp. 62–3.
2. John Walsh, 'John Wesley and the Community of Goods' in K. Robbins (ed.), *Protestant Evangelicalism*, Oxford: Blackwell, 1990, pp. 25ff.
3. John Walsh, *John Wesley: a Bicentennial Tribute*, London: Dr Williams's Trust, 1993.
4. B. S. Schlenther, *Queen of the Methodists*, Bishop Auckland: Durham Academic Press, 1997, pp. 104ff; F. Cook, *Selina, Countess of Huntingdon*, Edinburgh: Banner of Truth Trust, 2001, p. 275; John Wesley, *Letters*, ed. J. Telford, London: Epworth Press, 1960, vol. 5, pp. 211, 258.
5. V. H. H. Green, *John Wesley*, London: Nelson, 1964, p. 104.

1. After Wesley – the Era of Revolution 1791–1820

For this period see *A History of the Methodist Church in Great Britain*, ed. Rupert Davies and Gordon Rupp, London: Epworth Press, 1965–88 – vol. 1, ch. 9 by John Walsh; vol. 2, ch. 1 by W. R. Ward and ch. 7 by J. T. Wilkinson. See also J. C. Bowmer, *Pastor and People*, London: Epworth Press, 1975.

1. R. Currie *et al.*, *Churches and Churchgoers*, London: Oxford University Press, 1977; C. D. Field, 'The Social Composition of Methodism', *Bulletin of the John Rylands Library* 1994, pp. 151–65; C. D. Field, 'The Sociology of Methodism', *Journal of Sociology*, July 1977, pp. 119–225.
2. W. R. Ward, *Religion and Society in England 1790–1850*, London: Batsford, 1972, p. 1.
3. J. K. Lander, *Itinerant Temples: Tent Methodism 1814–1832*, Carlisle: Paternoster, 2003.
4. For the Sidmouth Bill see Ward, pp. 54–63; M. Batty, *Stages in the Development of Wesleyan Lay Leadership*, London: Methodist Publishing House, 1993, pp. 51ff; R. W. Davis, *Dissent in Politics 1780–1830*, London: Epworth Press, 1971, ch. 9; D. Hempton, *The Religion of the People: Methodism and Popular Religion, c. 1750–1900*, London: Routledge, 1996, ch. 6; B. L. Manning, *The Protestant Dissenting Deputies*, Cambridge: Cambridge University Press, 1952, pp. 130ff.
5. *Minutes* of Wesleyan Conference 1812, *The Presidential Address*.
6. Ward, pp. 93–4.
7. R. Anstey, *The Atlantic Slave Trade and British Abolition, 1760–1810*, London: Macmillan, 1975; N. Ferguson, *Empire: How Britain Made the Modern World*, London: Allen Lane, 2003.

2. The Era of Jabez Bunting 1820–60

1. T. W. Laqueur, *Religion and Respectability: Sunday Schools and Working Class Culture, 1780–1850*, London: Yale University Press, 1976; cf. E. P. Thompson,

The Making of the English Working Class, Harmondsworth: Penguin, 1968, especially ch. 11, pp. 385ff; Callum G. Brown, *The Death of Christian Britain: Understanding Secularisation 1800–2000*, London: Routledge, 2000.

2. Margaret Batty, *Stages in the Development and Control of Wesleyan Lay Leadership 1791–1878*, London: Methodist Publishing House, 1993, ch. 9; G. Milburn and M. Batty (eds), *Workaday Preachers*, London: Methodist Publishing House, 1995, ch. 2 by J. M. Turner. For the famous Bunting saying, see the *Nottingham Review* 14 December 1827.

3. Michael Edwards, *Purge This Realm: a Life of Joseph Rayner Stephens*, London: Epworth Press, 1994.

4. O. A. Beckerlegge, *The United Methodist Free Churches*, London: Epworth Press, 1957.

5. E. J. Hobsbawm, *The Age of Revolution*, London: New English Library, 1962, p. 245.

6. E. G. Rupp, *Thomas Jackson, Methodist Patriarch*, London: Epworth Press, 1954; M. Selén, *The Oxford Movement and Wesleyan Methodism in England 1833–1882*, Lund: Lund University Press, 1992.

7. Cf. recent articles by D. A. Burton (Derbyshire) and N. Virgoe (Norfolk) in *WHS Proceedings*, May, October 1999. Also R. F. Wearmouth, *Methodism and the Struggle of the Working Classes, 1850–1900*, Leicester: Edgar Backus, 1954, p. 91.

8. Ian Randall and David Hilborn, *One Body in Christ: the History and Significance of the Evangelical Alliance*, Carlisle: Paternoster, 2001.

9. D. L. Cooney, *The Methodists in Ireland*, Blackrock, Co. Dublin: Columba Press 2001; L. Madden (ed.), *Methodism in Wales: a Short History of the Wesley Tradition*, Llandudno: Methodist Conference, 2003.

10. M. Watts, *The Dissenters* vol. 2, Oxford: Clarendon Press, 1995; cf. K. D. M. Snell and Paul S. Ell, *Rival Jerusalems: the Geography of Victorian Religion*, Cambridge: Cambridge University Press, 2000.

3. *Victorian Values – What Was it Like to be a Wesleyan?*

1. H. B. Workman, *The Place of Methodism in the Catholic Church*, London: Epworth Press, 1921, pp. 16ff; D. W. Bebbington, *Holiness in Nineteenth Century England*, Carlisle: Paternoster, 2000.

2. T. Runyon, *The New Creation*, Nashville: Abingdon Press, 1998, pp. 146ff.

3. D. Hempton, *The Religion of the People: Methodism and Popular Religion, c. 1750–1900*, London: Routledge, 1996, p. 5.

4. H. J. Perkin, *The Origins of Modern English Society 1780–1880*, London: Routledge & Kegan Paul, 1969, pp. 340ff.

5. J. Kent, *Wesley and the Wesleyans*, Cambridge: Cambridge University Press, 2002, pp. 200ff.

6. P. S. Bagwell, *Outcast London: a Christian Response*, London: Epworth Press, 1987, p. 87.

7. R. A. Knox, *Enthusiasm*, Oxford: Clarendon Press, 1950, p. 449.

8. G. Milburn, 'Piety, Profit and Paternalism', *PWHS*, December 1983, pp. 45–69; D. J. Jeremy, *Capitalists and Christians: Business Leaders and the Churches in Britain 1900–60*, Oxford: Clarendon Press, 1990; D. J. Jeremy, *Religion, Business and Wealth in Modern Britain*, London: Routledge, 1998; J. Garnett, 'Nonconformists, Economic Ethics and the Consumer Society in Mid-Victorian Britain' in *Culture and the Nonconformist Tradition* ed. J. Shaw and A. Kreider, Cardiff: University of Wales Press, 1999, pp. 95–116; J. M. Gibbs, *Morels of Cardiff: a Family Shipping Firm*, Cardiff: Amgueddfa Genedlaethol Cymru, 1982.

9. T. MacQuiban, 'Friends of All? – The Wesleyan Response to Urban Poverty in Britain and Ireland 1780–1840' in *The Poor and the People Called Methodists* ed. R. P. Heitzenrater, Nashville: Abingdon Press, 2002.

10. M. Thatcher, *The Standard*, April 1983.

11. J. M. Turner, 'Conference, Local Preachers and the LPMA' in 'Preachers All' ed. D. C. Dews, *Yorkshire WHS*, 1987, pp. 23–32; A. Parker, *Confidence in Mutual Aid*, London: Methodist Publishing House, 1998.

12. G. T. Brake, *Drink: Ups and Downs of Methodist Attitudes to Temperance*, London: Oliphants, 1974; C. D. Field, 'The Devil in Solution: How Temperate Were Methodists?', *Epworth Review*, July 2000, pp. 79–93; B. Harrison, *Drink and the Victorians*, London: Faber, 1971.

13. R. Moore, *Pitmen, Preachers and Politics: the Effects of Methodism in a Durham Mining Community*, London: Cambridge University Press, 1974, p. 116; I have used here my lecture 'Victorian Values or Whatever Happened to John Wesley's Scriptural Holiness?', *PWHS*, October 1988, pp. 165–84.

4. Wesleyan Worship

1. J. C. Bowmer, *The Lord's Supper in Methodism 1791–1960*, London: Epworth Press, 1961; K. Westerfield Tucker, (ed.), *The Sunday Service of the Methodists*, Nashville: Abingdon Press, 1996, especially the chapter by A. R. George.

2. J. M. Turner, *Conflict and Reconciliation*, London: Epworth Press, 1985, p. 133; cf. F. Knight, *The Nineteenth Century Church and English Society*, Cambridge: Cambridge University Press, 1998, pp. 20ff.

3. J. Crowther, *A Portrait of Methodism*, London, 1815, pp. 271ff; A. Burdon, *The Preaching Service: the Glory of the Methodists*, Bramcote: Grove, 1991.

4. L. Madden (ed.), *Methodism in Wales: a Short History of the Wesley Tradition*, Llandudno: Methodist Conference, 2003, p. 75; cf. *PWHS* February 2000, pp. 39ff.

5. T. MacQuiban, 'A Prince Among Preachers – W. M. Punshon', *WHS Yorkshire*, September 1981.

6. G. Milburn and M. Batty (eds), *Workaday Preachers: the Story of Methodist Local Preaching*, Peterborough: Methodist Publishing House, 1995, p. 69; cf. ch. 2 by J. M. Turner and ch. 3 by G. Milburn.

7. D. Tripp, *The Renewal of the Covenant in the Methodist Tradition*, London: Epworth Press, 1969.

8. F. Baker, *Methodism and the Love Feast*, London: Epworth Press, 1957.

9. G. W. Dolbey, *The Architectural Expansion of Methodism*, London: Epworth Press, 1964; also needed to get a fuller picture: H. Davies, *Worship and Theology in England from Watts and Wesley to Maurice 1660–1850*, Oxford: Clarendon Press, 1961; G. Wakefield, *An Outline of Christian Worship*, Edinburgh: T and T Clark, 1998, ch. 7; J. F. White, *Protestant Worship*, Louisville, Ky: Westminster/John Knox Press, 1989.

10. P. T. Forsyth, *Christ on Parnassus*, London: Hodder and Stoughton, 1911, pp. 176ff.

5. Wesleyanism 1860–1902

1. M. Wellings, 'Making Haste Slowly. The Campaign for Lay Representation in the Wesleyan Conference 1871–8', *PWHS*, May 2001, pp. 25–37.

2. D. Carter, *Love Bade Me Welcome: a British Methodist Perspective on the Church*, London: Epworth Press, 2002, ch. 2; D. Carter, *James H. Rigg*, Peterborough: Foundery Press, 1994.

3. E. R. Wickham, *Church and People in an Industrial City*, London: Lutterworth Press, 1957, pp. 266ff; J. M. Todd, *John Wesley and the Catholic Church*, London: Hodder & Stoughton, 1958, p. 10.

4. J. T. Smith, *Methodism and Education, 1849–1902*, Oxford: Clarendon Press, 1998. J. N. Figgis, *Churches in the Modern State*, London: Longmans, Green, 1913, ch. 1.

5. *A History of the Methodist Church in Great Britain*, ed. Rupert Davies and Gordon Rupp, London: Epworth Press, 1965–88, vol. 3, ch. 8 by F. C. Pritchard.

6. D. Baker, *Partnership in Excellence*, Cambridge 1975. D. Martin, *A Sociology of English Religion*, London: Heinemann, 1967, p. 89.

7. E. D. Graham, *Saved to Serve: the Story of the Wesley Deaconess Order, 1890–1978*, Werrington: Methodist Publishing House, 2002.

8. C. Oldstone-Moore, *Hugh Price Hughes*, Cardiff: University of Wales Press, 1999; G. I. T. Machin, *Politics and the Churches in Great Britain 1869 to 1921*, Oxford: Clarendon Press, 1987; D. W. Bebbington, *The Nonconformist Conscience: Chapel and Politics, 1870-1914*, London: Allen and Unwin, 1982, esp. p. 11.

9. J. Banks, *The Story So Far: The First 100 Years of the Manchester and Salford Methodist Mission*, 1986.

10. W. Leary, *The Wesley Guild: the First Hundred Years*, 1996.

6. Wesleyanism 1902–32

1. *A History of the Methodist Church in Great Britain*, ed. Rupert Davies and Gordon Rupp, London: Epworth Press, 1965–88, vol. 3, chapters by H. D. Rack, W. Strawson, J. T. Wilkinson and J. M. Turner; also J. Munson, *The Nonconformists*, London: SPCK, 1991, p. 1.

2. A. Turberfield, *John Scott Lidgett*, Werrington: Epworth Press, 2003.

3. D. W. Bebbington, 'The Persecution of George Jackson' in *Persecution and Toleration* ed. W. J. Sheils, Oxford: Blackwell, 1984, pp. 421–33; M. Wellings, 'The Wesley Bible Union', *PWHS*, vol. 53, pt 5, May 2002, pp. 157–68.

4. A. Wilkinson, *Dissent or Conform? War, Peace and*

the English Churches, London: SCM Press, 1986; K. Robbins, 'Protestant Nonconformists and the Peace Question' in *Protestant Nonconformity in the Twentieth Century* ed. A. P. F. Sell and A. R. Cross, Carlisle: Paternoster, 2003, pp. 216–39.

5. D. Martin, *Pacifism: an Historical and Sociological Study*, London: Routledge & Kegan Paul, 1965; M. Hughes, 'Methodist Pacifism 1899–1939', *PWHS*, October 1902, pp. 203–14.

6. cf. J. Kent, *The Age of Disunity*, London: Epworth Press, 1965, pp. 1–43; R. Currie, *Methodism Divided*, London: Faber, 1968, pp. 217ff; A. J. Bolton, 'The Other Side – Opposition to Methodist Union 1913–1932', *PWMHS* 1994.

7. Eric Baker, *Fathers and Brethren*, London: Epworth Press, 1959 and later statements; *Methodist Recorder*, 24 July 1960.

7. The Wesleyans and Other Christians

1. D. W. Bebbington, *Evangelicalism in Modern Britain*, Unwin Hyman, 1989, pp. 2ff; M. A. Noll, *The Rise of Evangelicalism*, Leicester: IVP, 2004, pp. 14, 16.

2. F. K. Brown, *The Fathers of the Victorians: the Age of Wilberforce*, Cambridge: Cambridge University Press, 1961.

3. I. Randall and D. Hilborn, *One Body in Christ: the History and Significance of the Evangelical Alliance*, Carlisle: Paternoster, 2001.

4. C. Binfield, *George Williams and the YMCA*, London: Heinemann, 1973, p. 158.

5. P. B. Nockles, *The Oxford Movement in Context: Anglican High Churchmanship, 1760–1857*, Cambridge: Cambridge University Press, 1994.

6. J. M. Turner, *Conflict and Reconciliation*, London: Epworth Press, 1985, ch. 8. I have drawn much on this book in this chapter.

7. B. Heeney, *A Different Kind of Gentleman*, Archon Books, 1976; cf. F. Knight, *The Nineteenth Century Church and English Society*, Cambridge: Cambridge University Press, 1995.

8. J. Obelkevich, *Religion and Rural Society: South Lindsey 1825–1875*, Oxford: Clarendon Press, 1976, pp. 115ff, 164ff.

9. D. W. Bebbington, *The Nonconformist Conscience: Chapel and Politics 1870–1914*, London: Allen and Unwin, 1982, ch. 4; E. K. H. Jordan, *Free Church Unity*, London: Lutterworth Press, 1956; J. A. Newton, 'Protestant Nonconformity and Ecumenism' in *Protestant Nonconformity in the Twentieth Century* ed. A. P. F. Sell and A. R. Cross, Carlisle: Paternoster, 2003, pp. 357–80.

10. R. Rouse and S. C. Neill (eds), *A History of the Ecumenical Movement*, London: SPCK, 1967, pp. 353ff. A. G. M. Stephenson, *Anglicanism and the Lambeth Conferences*, London: SPCK, 1978.

Conclusion

1. E. J. Hobsbawm, *Age of Extremes: the Short Twentieth Century 1914–1991*, London: Michael Joseph, 1994, p. 3.

2. B. E. Beck, 'Some Reflections on Connexionalism', *Epworth Review*, May, September 1991; T. MacQuiban, 'Does Methodism Matter Enough?', *Epworth Review*, May 1996.

Further Reading

Essential

A History of the Methodist Church in Great Britain, ed. Rupert Davies and Gordon Rupp, London: Epworth Press, 1965–88, 4 vols. Chapters by J. Walsh (vol. 1), J. Kent (vol. 2), H. Rack and J. Turner (vol. 3) give a narrative, others deal with more special topics.

A Dictionary of Methodism in Britain and Ireland, ed. J. A. Vickers, Peterborough: Epworth Press, 2000.

General history

Best, G. F. A., *Mid-Victorian Britain 1851–1875*, London: Fontana, 1972.

Briggs, Asa, *The Age of Improvement 1783–1867*, London: Longmans, 1959, 1964; 2nd ed., Harlow: Longmans, 2000.

Christie, Ian R., *Wars and Revolutions: Britain 1760–1815*, London: Edward Arnold, 1982.

Clarke, Peter, *Hope and Glory: Britain, 1900–1990*, London: Allen Lane, 1996.

Harrison, J. F. C., *Early Victorian Britain 1832–1851*, London: Fontana, 1979.

Harrison, J. F. C., *Late Victorian Britain 1875–1901*, London: Fontana, 1990.

Hastings, Adrian, *A History of English Christianity 1920–1985*, London: Collins, 1986.

Mathias, P., *The First Industrial Nation*, London: Methuen, 1969.

Newsome, David, *The Victorian World Picture*, London: Fontana, 1997.

O'Gorman, Frank, *The Long Eighteenth Century: British Political and Social History, 1688–1832*, London: Arnold, 1997.

Perkin, H., *The Origins of Modern English Society 1780–1880*, London: Routledge & Kegan Paul, 1969.

Royle, Edward, *Modern Britain: a Social History, 1750–1997*, 2nd ed., London: Arnold, 1997.

Thompson, E. P., *The Making of the English Working Class*, Harmondsworth: Penguin, 1968.

Thompson, F. M. L., *The Rise of Respectable Society*, London: Fontana, 1988.

The churches from 1791 to 1932

These books make a comprehensive and varied introduction to the period from 1791 to 1932:

Bebbington, D. W., *Evangelicalism in Modern Britain*, Unwin Hyman, 1989.

Bebbington, D. W., *The Nonconformist Conscience: Chapel and Politics 1870–1914*, London: Allen and Unwin 1982.

Binfield, Clyde, *So Down to Prayers: Studies in English Nonconformity, 1780–1920*, London: Dent, 1977.

Briggs, J., and Sellers, I. (eds), *Protestant Nonconformity*, London: Arnold, 1973.

Chadwick, O., *The Victorian Church*, London: Black, 1966, 1970, 2 vols.

Clark, G. Kitson, *Churchmen and the Condition of England 1832–1885*, London: Macmillan, 1973.

Davies, E. T., *Religion in the Industrial Revolution in South Wales*, Cardiff: University of Wales Press, 1965.

Gilbert, Alan D., *Religion and Society in Industrial England: Church, Chapel and Social Change, 1740–1914*, London: Longman, 1976.

Gilley, S., and Sheils, W. J. (eds), *A History of Religion in Britain*, Oxford: Blackwell, 1994.

Hilton, Boyd, *The Age of Atonement: the Influence of Evangelicalism on Social and Economic Thought, 1795–1865*, Oxford: Clarendon Press, 1988.

Hole, Robert, *Pulpits, Politics and Public Order in England, 1760–1832*, Cambridge: Cambridge University Press, 1989.

Hylson-Smith, K., *The Churches in England from Elizabeth I to Elizabeth II*, vols 2 and 3, London: SCM Press, 1997, 1998.

Knight, Frances, *The Nineteenth-Century Church and English Society*, Cambridge: Cambridge University Press, 1995.

Machin, G. I. T., *Politics and the Churches in Great Britain, 1832 to 1868*, Oxford: Clarendon Press, 1977.

Machin, G. I. T., *Politics and the Churches in Great Britain, 1869 to 1921*, Oxford: Clarendon Press, 1987.

McLeod, Hugh, *Religion and the People of Western Europe 1789–1970*, Oxford: Oxford University Press, 1981.

McLeod, Hugh, *Religion and Society in England 1850–1914*, Basingstoke: Macmillan, 1996.

Munson, James, *The Nonconformists: In Search of a Lost Culture*, London: SPCK, 1991.

Norman, Edward, *The English Catholic Church in the Nineteenth Century*, Oxford: Clarendon Press, 1984.

Protestant Nonconformity in the Twentieth Century: a Retrospect, ed. Alan P. F. Sell and Anthony R. Cross, Carlisle: Paternoster, 2003.

Religion in Victorian Britain, ed. G. Parsons and J. R. Moore, Manchester:

Manchester University Press, 1988– , 5 vols. Full of meat – surveys and documents.

Rosman, Doreen, *The Evolution of the English Churches, 1500–2000*, Cambridge: Cambridge University Press, 2003.

Snell, K. D. M., and Ell, Paul S., *Rival Jerusalems: the Geography of Victorian Religion*, Cambridge: Cambridge University Press, 2000.

Thompson, D. M., *Nonconformity in the Nineteenth Century*, London: Routledge & Kegan Paul, 1972.

Ward, W. R., *Religion and Society in England, 1790–1850*, London: Batsford, 1972.

Watts, Michael R., *The Dissenters*, vol 2, *The Expansion of Evangelical Nonconformity*, Oxford: Clarendon Press, 1995.

Recent specific studies

Bagwell, Philip S., *Outcast London: a Christian Response: the West London Mission of the Methodist Church 1887–1987*, London: Epworth Press, 1987.

Barritt, Gordon E., *Thomas Bowman Stephenson*, Peterborough: Foundery Press, 1996.

Batty, Margaret, *Stages in the Development and Control of Wesleyan Lay Leadership 1791–1878*, London: Methodist Publishing House, 1988.

Bowmer, John C., *Pastor and People: a Study of Church and Ministry in Wesleyan Methodism from the Death of Wesley (1791) to the Death of Jabez Bunting (1858)*, London: Epworth Press, 1975.

Bunting, Jabez, *The Early Correspondence of Jabez Bunting 1820–1829*, ed. W. R. Ward, London: Royal Historical Society, 1972.

Bunting, Jabez, *Early Victorian Methodism: the Correspondence of Jabez Bunting 1830–1858*, ed. W. R. Ward, Oxford: Oxford University Press, 1976.

Bunting, Jabez, *Scottish Methodism in the Early Victorian Period: the Scottish Correspondence of the Rev. Jabez Bunting 1800–57* ed. A. J. Hayes and D. A. Gowland, Edinburgh: Edinburgh University Press, 1981.

Carter, David, *James H. Rigg*, Peterborough: Foundery Press, 1994.

Carter, David, *Love Bade Me Welcome: a British Methodist Perspective on the Church*, Peterborough: Epworth Press, 2002.

Cooney, Dudley Levistone, *The Methodists in Ireland: a Short History*, Blackrock, Co. Dublin: Columba Press, 2001.

Currie, R., *Methodism Divided*, London: Faber, 1968.

Davies, R. E., *Methodism*, 2nd ed., London: Epworth Press, 1985.

Edwards, Michael S., *S. E. Keeble: the Rejected Prophet*, Chester: Wesley Historical Society, 1977.

Gowland, D. A., *Methodist Secessions: the Origins of Free Methodism in Three Lancashire Towns: Manchester, Rochdale, Liverpool*, Manchester: Manchester University Press, 1979.

Howarth, D. H., *The Story of Samuel Chadwick*, Cliff College, 1983.

Hempton, David, *Methodism and Politics in British Society 1750–1850*, London: Hutchinson, 1984.

Hempton, David, *The Religion of the People: Methodism and Popular Religion, c. 1750–1900*, London: Routledge, 1996.

Kent, John, *The Age of Disunity*, London: Epworth Press, 1966.

Kent, John, *Holding the Fort: Studies in Victorian Revivalism*, London: Epworth Press, 1978.

Madden, Lionel (ed.), *Methodism in Wales: a Short History of the Wesley Tradition*, Llandudno: Methodist Conference, 2003.

Meadley, T. D., *The Story of Thomas Champness*, Cliff College, 1983.

Milburn, Geoffrey, *Primitive Methodism*, Peterborough: Epworth Press, 2003.

Oldstone-Moore, Christopher, *Hugh Price Hughes: Founder of a New Methodism, Conscience of a New Nonconformity*, Cardiff: University of Wales Press, 1999.

Pawson, John, *The Letters of John Pawson: Methodist Itinerant, 1762–1806*, ed. John C. Bowmer and John A. Vickers, Peterborough: Methodist Publishing House, 1994–5, 3 vols.

Sails, G., *At the Centre: the Story of Methodism's Central Missions*, Home Mission Department, 1970.

Semmel, B., *The Methodist Revolution*, London: Heinemann, 1977.

Smith, John T., *Methodism and Education, 1849–1902: J. H. Rigg, Romanism, and Wesleyan Schools*, Oxford: Clarendon Press, 1998.

Tabraham, Barrie W., *The Making of Methodism*, London: Epworth Press, 1995.

Taggart, Norman W., *William Arthur: First among Methodists*, London: Epworth Press, 1997.

Turberfield, Alan, *John Scott Lidgett*, Werrington: Epworth Press, 2003.

Turner, John Munsey, *Conflict and Reconciliation: Studies in Methodism and Ecumenism in England 1740–1982*, London: Epworth Press, 1985.

Turner, John Munsey, *John Wesley: the Evangelical Revival and the Rise of Methodism in England*, Peterborough: Epworth Press, 2002.

Wakefield, Gordon S., *Methodist Spirituality*, Peterborough: Epworth Press, 1999.

Ward, W. R., *Faith and Faction*, London: Epworth Press, 1993, chapters 12–15.

Workaday Preachers: the Story of Methodist Local Preaching, ed. Geoffrey Milburn and Margaret Batty, Peterborough: Methodist Publishing House, 1995.

Some local histories

Cox, Jeffrey, *The English Churches in a Secular Society: Lambeth 1870–1930*, Oxford: Oxford University Press, 1982.

Clark, David, *Between Pulpit and Pew: Folk Religion in a North Yorkshire Fishing Village*. Cambridge: Cambridge University Press, 1982.

Crofts, Bruce (ed.), *At Satan's Throne: Methodism in Bath*, Bristol: White Tree, 1990.

Green, S. J. D., *Religion in the Age of Decline: Organisation and Experience in Industrial Yorkshire, 1870–1920*, Cambridge: Cambridge University Press, 1996.

Hargreaves, John A., *Halifax*, Edinburgh: Edinburgh University Press, 1999.

Mason, Alistair (ed.), *Religion in Leeds*, Stroud: Alan Sutton, 1994.

Milburn, G., *Church and Chapel in Sunderland 1830–1914*, University of Sunderland, 1988.

Moore, Robert, *Pitmen, Preachers and Politics: the Effects of Methodism in a Durham Mining Community*, London: Cambridge University Press, 1974.

Obelkevich, James, *Religion and Rural Society: South Lindsey, 1825–1875*, Oxford: Clarendon Press, 1976.

Robson, G., *Dark Satanic Mills: Religion and Irreligion in Birmingham and the Black Country*, Carlisle: Paternoster, 2003.

Rose, E. A., *Methodism in Ashton-under-Lyne*, Ashton: E. A. Rose, 1969.

Royle, Edward, *Nonconformity in Nineteenth-Century York*, York: St Anthony's Press, 1985.

Royle, E., *Queen Street Chapel and Mission, Huddersfield*, Huddersfield, 1994.

Scotland, Nigel, *Methodism and the Revolt of the Field: a Study of the Methodist contribution to Agricultural Trade Unionism in East Anglia 1872–96*, Gloucester: Sutton, 1981.

Shaw, Thomas, *A History of Cornish Methodism*, Truro: D. Bradford Barton, 1967.

Smith, Mark, *Religion in Industrial Society: Oldham and Saddleworth, 1740–1865*, Oxford: Clarendon Press, 1994.

Stubley, Peter, *A House Divided: Evangelicals and the Establishment in Hull, 1770–1914*, Hull: University of Hull Press, 1995.

Tomkins, D., *The Story of the First 100 Years of Bolton Methodist Mission*, Bolton, 1997.

Vickers, J. A., *The Story of Canterbury Methodism (1750–1961)*, Harbledown: St Peter's Methodist Trust, 1961.

Yeo, Stephen, *Religion and Voluntary Organisations in Crisis*, London: Croom Helm, 1976 (about Reading, Berks.).

Older books by E. R. Taylor, M. Edwards and R. F. Wearmouth are still worth reading. There are many more local studies. Explore your local archives for histories of Methodist chapels.

The *Proceedings of the Wesley Historical Society* from 1893 are an essential source, as is the *Epworth Review* and an earlier periodical *The London Quarterly and Holborn Review*.

Index